D1464794

COME OUT
THE WILDERNESS

BRUCE KENRICK, a war-time paratroop officer and member of the Iona Community, is a graduate of Edinburgh University and of Princeton Theological Seminary. His work in West Bengal with the United Church of Northern India, and in the East Harlem Protestant Parish described in this book, gave rise to the 'theology of identification' which he set out in *The New Humanity* (1957). Mr. Kenrick is continuing this work today as a minister in a multi-racial area of London where he is Chairman of the Notting Hill Housing Trust.

by the same author
THE NEW HUMANITY

BRUCE KENRICK

Come Out the Wilderness

We feel like a-shoutin' as we
Come out the wilderness,
Leanin' on the Lord.
    —NEGRO SPIRITUAL

Collins

FONTANA BOOKS

First published by Wm. Collins & Sons, Ltd., 1962
First issued in Fontana Books, 1965
Second Impression, February 1965
Third Impression, September 1965

TO MY FATHER
WITH GRATITUDE

CONDITIONS OF SALE: *This book shall not be lent,
re-sold, hired out or otherwise disposed of by way
of trade in any form of binding or cover other
than that in which it is published*

*The drawing on the cover
is by Joseph Papin*

© *Bruce Kenrick, 1962*
Printed in Great Britain
Collins Clear-Type Press
London and Glasgow

CONTENTS

Contents

PART FIVE *Strange Pilgrimage*

PART SIX *The Divine Guarantee*

INTRODUCTION

For me, the most poignant moment and memory of *West Side Story* was that in the drug-store where one of the gangs used to meet. The old store-keeper, so obviously sympathetic and kindly, is at last exasperated beyond endurance and flings out: 'You know you fellers make this world lousy!' And one of the boys replies: 'We found it that way.'

Bruce Kenrick, in this account of a magnificent Christian experiment in East Harlem makes it plain in every line of what he writes that it is the world *as it is*, men and women *where they are* that the church must reach. In this way he is in fact giving expression to one of the most profound truths of the Christian faith: the truth that God also cares enough for man to come where he is. That is what the word 'incarnation' really means. And because the church is the extension of the incarnation, the continuing activity of Christ in the world, it can only be itself if it, too, comes to find man where he is.

East Harlem, at least at the time when the East Harlem Protestant Parish began its existence, was entirely typical of those parts of the world where men live who have been cast off by the affluent society. It could, I imagine, be easily paralleled in every great city of the modern world. Certainly I could recognise again and again the streets, the rooms, the people—and sometimes the tone of voice—that I used to know so well in the African slums of Johannesburg.

There are certain qualities about this book which make it, for me anyhow, a great experience.

It is not so surprising that it should be compassionate (though indeed it is that in full measure) about the problems and the tragedies it describes. Clearly, without compassion, there could be no Christian contact at all. But the stimulating and challenging thing about this book is its humility. Here is a great and glorious adventure: an attempt, in a new and exciting fashion, to reach people that the church quite clearly had failed to reach at all. Here, too, and unmistakably are the signs that this experiment, by God's grace, is working and is achieving a 'break-through'. Yet, over and over again the author is concerned to point out the mistakes, the failures, even the scandals, which the group knows itself to have provoked or shared. There is no attempt to over-persuade: no attempt to sentimentalise: no attempt to arouse compassion by a false emphasis on human frailty. And I cannot help thinking that it is this humility honesty if you prefer it, which gives the experiment its true strength.

Again, it is the way in which, by returning to discover fundamental meaning in what has become largely external formality in worship, the group discovers also the principle of its action, that is so stirring. There is no incongruity, but rather a perfect fitness, in the description of a simple parish communion alongside the social and political action which 'the parish' is involved in for the sake of its people. It is as if Christ's words, '. . . ye also should wash one another's feet . . .' are understood always in the context in which they were first spoken, the context of the Eucharist itself. And it becomes clear, as one reads this book, that Bible and Sacrament, Christian community and society as a whole, Heaven and East Harlem are so closely connected that they cannot be thought of in isolation from each other. If the Gospel is to be understood by those for whom it is meant, the gangster, the dope-addict, the prostitute, it must be *seen* to be relevant in the lives of those who proclaim it.

These men and women of whom Bruce Kenrick writes, and who initiated this great experiment, finally rejected the word 'identification' to express their way of approach: they feel, quite rightly, that this word should be reserved to the God who, laying aside his glory, was born in a manger and died on a cross. They preferred the word 'participation' as being more truly expressive of all they were trying to do. And certainly, in reading the story, it is evident that each and every one of them became part of East Harlem at the deepest level: and it was *from* this participation that their true strength as evangelists flowed.

But for our day perhaps the most significant factor of all is that of their unity. Not only that they represented eight different Christian communions, with all that that means of mutual charity and trust; but that, with this diverse background, they were able to make such a direct and compelling challenge in the name of the one Christ to a place like East Harlem: itself so diverse and divided by race and colour and creed.

Introduction

There is no need in fact for a preface to such a book as this. For where the Gospel is so obviously seen to be lived by those who preach it, what work is left for comment?

Here, for our post-Christian world, is an encouragement and a challenge beyond words: truly beyond words.

TREVOR HUDDLESTON C.R.
Bishop of Masasi
September, 1964

PART ONE

VENTURE INTO THE WILDERNESS

1. OUTPOST

The most exhilarating fact about East Harlem is that here, among so many disillusioned, broken men, a strong, confident community has taken root and grown. It is challenging, of course, to meet the band of pioneers who began it all by making their homes amid such chaos. And it is disturbing to have to face their unorthodox approach to those whose life they share. But what grips the imagination most is that this group has not perished in the wilderness but has built four vital, multi-racial congregations whose influence extends from the lives of ordinary men to those of local gangleaders and out beyond their corner of New York to Washington and the President's committees.

To glimpse one source of their strength:

A drug addict sits on the front bench in the small storefront church which was once a butcher's shop. At his side is a coloured man just out of jail. Behind them is the Cruz family, an asset to any neighbourhood. Near the back sits a well-dressed, middle-aged prostitute.

The benches are packed with Puerto Ricans, Negroes, and Italians; among them men and women who would never normally enter a church: the drunk, the thief, the outcast of society. Just the kind of company Jesus kept.

It is time for the prayer of intercession, and the minister, in light grey robe, asks, 'What prayers shall we offer God today?' There is a pause. Then a Puerto Rican on relief stands up: 'The landlord promised the Christian Action group he'd fix the plumbing in Betsie's apartment. Signed the statement, too. We ought to thank God.' Another pause. Then twenty-year-old Josh is on his feet: 'Maybe we could pray for the families who'll be baptised next week?' Old Luigi rises, leaning heavily on his stick: 'Supposin' there was another gang fight like last night. I mean just supposin'. It'd be good if no one else got killed. I'm not sayin' anythin' about anybody. I'm just sayin' it'd be good if no one else got killed, that's all.' The uneasy stir is broken by another voice. And another. Then: ' Let us pray.'

The pastor turns to the white communion table, looks up at the wooden cross that hangs on the deep-red wall, and then he kneels to offer the prayers of the courageous, the strong, the rejected, the weak, the despised: those who, together, are discovering how social and spiritual chaos can be fought and overcome.

How did this colourful community emerge? It all began just after the Second World War in the mind of an infantry ex-serviceman, the down-to-earth, imaginative Don Benedict.

2. 'THIS IS WHERE I BELONG'

Benedict had once shared a prison cell with a Trotskyite and a volume of Reinhold Niebuhr's ethics. Between the two, he was converted from pacifism in 1943 and was released when he agreed to register for call-up. He sailed west as a burly first sergeant, and soon his resourcefulness and gifts of leadership were tested and proved in action in the Pacific.

Now in the autumn of 1947 he was a final year divinity student, and, sitting in the chapel of New York's Union Theological Seminary, he was frankly perplexed. His problem was the writing on the great central window; for the words were a command: ' Go ye into all the world, and preach the gospel to every creature.' And Benedict was baffled by a strange discrepancy. Religion in America was thriving. New York had literally thousands of churches, mostly very much alive. But the most densely populated district in the city had been virtually abandoned by the church. ' Go ye into *all* the world. . . .' Seminary graduates were responding to the writing on the window by going out to India and Africa and to most of America, and none would question that they were right to go. But a few blocks away from the tranquil chapel, between Fifth Avenue and the East River, was an almost entirely neglected ' continent ' seething with social outcasts and frustrated, hopeless men. The U. S. Public Health Service had called it ' The Hell of Manhattan '. Officially, its title was East Harlem.

Benedict had been both attracted and repelled by the district. He knew that the problems facing the church there were immense, overwhelming, and fundamentally just the same as those which faced it everywhere. But here they were caricatured; they were on show for all to see; nothing was hidden. To walk through the district was to be exposed to a tragedy compounded of the Fall in the Garden of Eden, the chaos in the Tower of Babel, and the pain of the Crucifixion. How to change all this? How to make the Gospel come alive in such confusion? The problem shouted at the passer-by and echoed back and forth among the grey tenement dwellings. Benedict was uncomfortably convinced that the answer was being shouted at him too.

He left the chapel determined to work out the beginnings of the answer that had gripped him. But before he did so, he made a thoroughgoing survey of the district. In this he was joined by a fellow student who, like himself, was a Congregationalist; this was Bill Webber—a lean, intense, ex-naval officer with a crew haircut and a forthright manner. Webber had grown up in the placid social currents of Des Moines, Iowa, but spent much of the war on a destroyer hunting Nazi submarines in the Atlantic. He and Benedict made a likeable and formidable pair.

Together they tramped back and forth through East Harlem's streets and made their first descriptive notes:

Six-storey cold-water tenements with mouldering fire escapes. Garbage everywhere: ashcans filled to overflowing: fires burning in the gutter and on vacant lots. Broken glass on the street. Radios blaring. Small boys rushing out in front of speeding cars. Sidewalks teeming —Negroes, Puerto Ricans, Italians, Jews. A bleak empty space where a house has been torn down, leaving bricks and a grotesque iron bedstead, rusted and projecting out of the rubble. Small children in flimsy clothes play gaily among the debris; their bright smiles are a contrast to their elder brothers' cynical attitude. No wonder.

The two men were getting the feel of the district. They went calling and learned so much that for a while even Benedict's infectious laugh was silenced. In one tenement they found twenty-seven persons (including seventeen children and an eight-day-old infant) housed in four basement coalhouses; each grimy cubicle was renting for $40 a month: the landlord was pastor of a nearby storefront church. They took notes of complaints as their survey progressed:

Petra Fernandez, aged 80, 62 East 100th Street, Apart. 14. 'This kitchen door is hanging by one nail. It'll fall on me one day. I'm not paying rent till the landlord fixes it.'

Juan Jimenez, 211 East 106th Street, Apart. 4 W. 'See the ceiling; it's falling down. And the toilet's dropping sideways through the boards. If I sit on it, I'll go right through the floor.'

Gradually, general impressions were reinforced by solid facts. They wrote:

East Harlem is one of the world's most densely populated areas, as well as the most crowded section of an already overcrowded city. Extending from 96th Street to 125th Street, and bounded on the west by Central Park and on the east by the East River, it is a jumble of seething humanity and decrepit houses. More than 200,000 people live jammed together in little over one square mile. On one block more than 4,000 people are packed into 27 rotting tenements. Often several families live in one apartment. If all the inhabitants of the United States lived as close together as the people in East Harlem, they could be housed in one-half the area of New York City.

Immigrant waves of Irish, Italians, Russian Jews, Puerto Ricans, and Negroes have descended on East Harlem, and as the main body of the wave has passed on into suburbia, it has left behind in the district a few who like it and regard it as their home, and a multitude who hate it and regard it as their jail. Today, the population is made up mainly of Negroes, Puerto Ricans, and Italians in roughly equal numbers, but the faces of almost every nation and race can be seen in its densely crowded streets.

East Harlem has the highest rate in the city for T.B., V.D., infant mortality, rat bites, malnutrition. The trash and garbage disposal services are hopelessly inadequate. Many children are not wanted, and rarely go to school. Unmarried mothers are faced with the problem of supporting their families and themselves. Both young and old are on the borderline of crime or right in among it. Boys and girls are using dope.

So in that autumn of 1947 they began to build a realistic picture of life in this corner of the City of New York. They discovered that in winter the bitter cold invaded many apartments where the heating plants were out of order. In summer the days were scorching and the nights were steaming, for the concrete held the heat and made each day more stifling than the last; apartments were far too hot for the people to spend much time indoors, so the street was often teeming with a multi-racial crowd. Whether it was summer or whether it was winter, there was this congestion—and there was loneliness as well. Most next-door neighbours never even greeted one another. Benedict met two Puerto Rican families who had lived together in three rooms for six months without knowing each other's last names. 'East Harlem is a wilderness,' he wrote, 'a wilderness where the lonely crowd jostle each other unknowingly. . . .'

In this wilderness they touched on a few of the surface problems: housing, rubbish, tuberculosis. Some of these were to be banished with the years. But there were other problems that were infinitely worse, problems that remain today.

Benedict and Webber's understanding of these questions was soon acutely sharpened when they were joined by a man who really understood the issues from within.

Archie Hargraves was a Negro. He had grown up during the depression in North Carolina and moved to Harlem in the thirties. There he often went hungry for weeks, but despite almost incredible handicaps, he worked his way through college, got a job on the *Amsterdam News,* and with the coming of the war, he volunteered for the army and served as an officer in India. A square-set man with a deliberate manner and a friendly smile, he was now a graduate of a Baptist theological college and determined that the Gospel should come alive for the people among whom he had once lived.

Hargraves had no illusions about the choices open to East Harlem's people. He knew that a tiny minority maintained the struggle with dignity and built family lives that were precious islands in a sea of instability. But he also knew that most residents drifted down one of two steep paths.

There were a few who despite their inability to build a normal life still found the strength to strike out at society. Sometimes their object was both revenge and profit: their actions ranged from snatching handbags to shooting storekeepers and bank messengers for money. Often the object was more simple. A nineteen-year-old Puerto Rican was out on 100th Street, leaning through a car window and talking to a friend, when another Puerto Rican came by and knifed him in the back: he fell to the ground, gravely wounded. Neither had seen the other before. This was just revenge: blind, purposeless, illogical revenge against a society which seemed to be a fierce, implacable enemy.

But if a few lived self-respecting lives and others took to violence and crime, the great majority simply drifted. They had been so broken by a hostile world that there was no fight left in them. They were trapped in a crazy circle of helplessness from which the main ' escapes ' were either dope or sex or drink.

Dope led directly to crimes of theft and murder, for the addict had to get more than $5,000 a year with which to meet his need ; sex led to illegitimate, unwanted children, born with a grudge against the world ; and drink soaked up half of the family's Welfare money and plunged men deeper into the depths of despair, forcing them to seek another refuge, any refuge. But where? *Was* there any realistic refuge to be found? Easy enough to say, ' Let God be your refuge.' But, faced with such overwhelming frustrations, one could understand men asking, ' Is the Gospel big enough for this?'

The three ex-servicemen believed that it was. And the costly way in which they put their faith to work was inspired by the kind of fierce reproach which a student friend of Webber's met with on 100th Street.

He was helping with the Sunday calling programme, and was knocking for the third time on a grimy apartment door. There was the sound of shuffling feet inside, and then the door was opened by an unshaven Negro who had probably been wakened from his sleep on a battered couch. He stared at his visitor suspiciously, and then let him enter the shambles of a living room where his four small girls and naked year-old son were playing on the bare boards. The boy had a painful, wheezing cough ; he was asthmatic, said his father. There was an uneasy silence. It was broken by the man's listless voice explaining how his wife had deserted him the previous night, taking what money they had, and leaving him $70 worth of bills to pay. The doctor had said that the boy ought to see a specialist. This time the silence was longer.

Maybe the story was not true at all; but maybe it was. Certainly the picture in the room was true—a well-clothed, well-fed student of divinity, and a ragged, mixed-up Negro with a naked, coughing son. Still the silence was unbroken. The visitor was desperately groping for something helpful to say. But there was nothing in his experience, and least of all in his theological training, that spoke to this man's plight. Half wondering if he should simply hold his tongue, he began to stammer out some words of comfort from the Gospel—of how God really cared for this man in his need, of how God was in it with him. But he was cut short by the scorching rebuke, ' Yes, I know, you teach this stuff about life. But we have to *live* it!'

That was the crux of the matter. ' We have to live it!' And the work of the East Harlem Protestant Parish was born out of the conviction that only by living itself into the life of East Harlem could the church learn how to bring the Gospel to men like this resentful Negro.

' We saw,' said Webber later, ' that neither our enthusiasm, nor our bright ideas, nor our compassion for East Harlem were of much avail. There was no way out by methods of evangelism or by new organisations.' The one way out was by entering right into the heart of East Harlem's tensions, and from that position of physical involvement, learning how to be ministers of Christ.

The three summed up this basic conviction in the one word *identification*. Identification would mean living in the same kind of apartment and amid the same garbage as others in East Harlem. It would mean taking their families along, and exposing their children to the same temptations as the children who lived next door. It would mean being always at the disposal of the people with whom they sought identity, always having an open door, always responding to a visitor's knock, however late in the night it might come; it would mean, in other words, an abandonment of privacy and a free welcome into their family circle for the drug addict and the drunks and the friendless and the thieves. Identification with East Harlem would mean looking down the dismal streets and saying, ' This is my home; this is where I belong.'

This was, of course, what Christ had done on the first

Christmas Day when he came right down into the dirt of the stable in order to be *with* men, to share with them their loneliness, their tensions, and their rats, and from that position to offer his Good News. No doubt this was a way that might lead his disciples beyond Christmas Day to the darkness of Good Friday; but it might also be the one sure way that would lead to Easter Sunday.

'But you'll never last here,' a young man told Don Benedict. 'Anyone who wasn't born here couldn't learn to stand it.'

'You may be right,' came the thoughtful answer. 'You may very well be right.'

3. ONE MAN'S FRONTIER FIGHT

The one big problem to be solved before the three men put their faith to the test was: How to win the backing of their churches? This would call for clear-cut proposals based on serious research in East Harlem. They had to break through the important but superficial crust of housing and health and rubbish disposal problems to the heart of a hostile world that was torn up into helpless, near-demented fragments—like the family of Edward Washington.

Sitting on the steps of his house with Hargraves or Benedict or Webber, Ed Washington gave them what was, in effect, a course in sociology. He was an unkempt Negro with a disjointed way of speaking and an uneasy manner which he had acquired during ten years in East Harlem. He had come from the South with his wife and four children to the ' city of opportunity ' with great hopes of starting life anew. But at once he discovered that the freedom and equality of the North were more theories than realities. At least in the South he had known where he was ; but here discrimination was apt to hit him when he least expected it, and he found himself completely at the mercy of forces he could not begin to understand, dependent on vast, impersonal institutions.

The Housing Authority could wipe out the block where he lived and shatter those frail friendships which he might at last be making. The labour market's unpredictable swings made employment continually uncertain. The great city hospitals could admit his sick child or they could reject him. Everywhere giant institutions seemed to make illogical, confusing demands. In reporting housing violations, he might have to contact eleven different agencies ; he would have to report a leak in the gas stove to the Department of Housing and Buildings, a leak in the gas refrigerator to the Department of Health. And if he actually plucked up courage to make such a report, his coloured skin seemed to guarantee unsympathetic treatment from city institutions which seemed hostile and harsh and cruel.

Likewise the Washingtons were dismayed by the powerful

local forces which also seemed arrayed against them. 'They live,' as Hargraves put it later, 'in a neighbourhood run by gangsters, by cheating landlords, and by cops on the beat who ignore the dope peddler and beat up kids for being fresh.'

Loan sharks soon had the chance to take advantage of them; so did the landlord who could ignore the law and eject them whether they had been tenants for a week or twenty years. The racketeers seemed to control almost every aspect of life, and even death itself. A neighbour's twelve-year-old boy died of cancer, and less than an hour afterwards, when the parents had just returned from the hospital, a local undertaker mingled with the sympathising friends. He singled out the father and persuaded the heartbroken man to sign an $800 contract for the funeral. The father was a part-time docker; the mother eked out the family income by pasting pieces of coloured glass into jewellery frames. The undertaker put the contract in his pocket and drove off in his Cadillac.

So Ed Washington, overawed by the power and apparent indifference of the city's institutions, felt increasingly helpless and afraid in the presence of the local racketeers. He had begun to suspect that there was literally no one he could trust. Not even the police.

On arrival in the district he had talked with the small boy next door. 'What do you want to be when you grow up, son?' he asked. 'A cop?' 'A cop!' the boy exclaimed bitterly. 'Gee, no. I want to be a fireman. Firemen aren't like cops. They *save* people.' Soon Washington heard that some of the police were in league with the dope pushers; that some of them helped themselves to goods from local shops as a price for continued 'protection'; and that their methods with suspected criminals were sometimes unspeakably brutal. 'When the cops make an arrest, their policy is: Beat 'em up if they talk, and beat 'em up if they don't,' said a teenager to Washington after spending an evening in a local precinct house. 'I was hit in the stomach and I doubled up; then they hit me in the back of the neck 'til I fell. Then they kicked me, kept on kicking me—all over.' 'What we need,' said a local chemist, 'is not protection by the police, but protection *from* the police.' 'Where can I turn,' asked Washington, 'when I can't trust even the cops?' So dismay gave way to bitterness; and bitterness gave way to hate.

But beneath this hatred of city institutions and of local racketeers and police were deeper, more immediate hatreds which turned East Harlem into so many hostile camps. The most obvious and the most terrible of these were the camps that were based on colour. The whites, for example, were in one camp, taking their stand against Negroes and Puerto Ricans, however pale their skins might be. Next door to the Washington family was a Puerto Rican woman married to a Negro. She confided in Mrs. Washington, 'One of my kids came into the store and a white woman beside me said, "When you see these kids who aren't white or black or anything, you don't know where you are." I was so choked up I didn't know what to do.' And she continued, 'When folks find out I've a mixed marriage, they shout at my kids, "I don't know if you're black or white, but get to hell out of here."'

In another camp were the Puerto Ricans, standing against all Negroes. And the camp of the Negroes was standing against the world. Their children learned the terrible chant:

If you're white, you're all right,
If you're brown, hang around.
If you're black . . . stay back.

Sometimes the demon invaded the home. Archie Hargraves called on a family which lived just above the Washingtons. A Negro was cursing his Italian stepson for failing to take the day's garbage down to the bins at the front of the building. 'Take it down, Miguel, you hear me,' he yelled. 'Like hell I will,' said Miguel. 'It's your turn, God damn you!' came the protest. And the biting answer from his own stepson, 'Don't you cuss at me, you skin-dirty louse!' So racial prejudice poisoned almost every sphere of life. Even the language of religion seemed to mock the coloured man. 'Wash me,' came the revival hymn through the door of a Pentecostal storefront church. 'Wash me, and I shall be whiter than snow.' It seemed as though black was the colour of evil, and only the skins of the saints were white.

So the Washingtons' dream of a life set free from race discrimination turned slowly to a nightmare in a prison of racial hate. It seemed that whether your group was white or black or in between, it hated and was hated, it feared and was feared, it fought and was fought.

The Washingtons could have tolerated their separation from society at large and from other groups within East Harlem if only their own group had been a united community. It was not. With some outstanding exceptions, it was a group of bewildered rootless men. And the reasons were fairly clear. Their home was neither in East Harlem nor in the South. They had lost their own traditions and had none to take their place. Moreover, their group, like other groups, was atomised by the constant shift in population, for its members were always either moving house or being moved by the authorities. They were not even drawn together by having a common place of work, a common source of income, common trade unions, common strikes; instead their places of employment were scattered throughout the city, and were almost as numerous as the working members of the group themselves.

But a deeper reason for estrangement within the group was the unceasing competition for work and for homes. Jobs were few and apartments were fewer. Some people shared four rooms among three families, and every new arrival meant they had less chance to expand. So when the Washingtons arrived so full of expectation, they were at once surrounded by suspicion and mistrust. There was no welcome for them: not even from their own race. How could there be when they represented one more threat to the next man's apartment, to his pay packet, to his meat and drink? Apart from the few strong, stable families, each man was at war with his neighbour and his neighbourhood; and his neighbour and his neighbourhood were at war with him.

' But at least,' one might say hopefully, ' the Washingtons were together in these tensions. If they belonged neither to New York nor to East Harlem nor to their Negro neighbours, at least they belonged to one another.' ' Yes,' said Ed Washington when Benedict made this point, ' we did. But not for long.'

Benedict was learning what he meant. Ed and Henrietta Washington carried deep down inside them the memory of

the comparative security of a small share-cropping farm-
stead in the South. But while the parents tried to cling to
their old ways, their sons and daughters, growing up on city
streets, imbibed the general sense of insecurity, frustration,
mistrust. Both Ed and Henrietta were obliged to look for
work ; sometimes they found it, but when they did, long hours
away from home meant that they saw little of their children.
Like many other mothers, Henrietta had to tie the apartment
key around small Matthew's neck so that he could come in off
the street from time to time through the day. As Matthew
grew into a teenager, he found other places where he could
sleep, and often would not see his parents for days and nights
at a time. Soon he had little wish to see them, for their
lives were moving from bewilderment and hatred to abysmal
depths of despair. Matthew grew up with a sense of defeat
from the start because he saw only beaten men around him,
men with no fight left in them ; men like his father.

For ten frustrating years Ed Washington had lived more
off relief than off wages. For most of that time he had shared
four rooms with another growing family. Again and again
his poor education and his ignorance of city ways had made
him an easy prey for loan sharks and other racketeers. And
all the time, it seemed to him, the district grew more hostile,
more merciless, more menacing. Adultery was his confused
protest, his way of trying to affirm his manhood, of trying to
cloak his own inadequacy. It failed, as everything else had
failed ; and it brought disintegration right into the heart of
the home.

So amid the blare of radios and the merciless din of the
street, in miserable hallways where the dope pusher lurked
and neighbours passed without a smile, in a crowded apartment without the least pretence at privacy, where agonising
tensions never eased—here Edward Emmanuel Washington
was thrown back on his crumbling resources, and in the end
he fell apart.

4. THE CHURCH IRRELEVANT

Was the church doing anything at all to relieve this chaotic situation? Don Benedict was convinced that the answer was virtually ' No.' He had a theory, and he wanted to put it to the test. He knew that the reason normally given for the Protestant churches' departure from the slums was simply that the inhabitants had become Roman Catholic. Benedict suspected that this was no more than a comforting myth.

One warm Sunday morning he and another divinity student stationed themselves at either end of an East Harlem block. Here two thousand people lived; about half of them were Negroes, who are traditionally faithful Protestants, and half were Puerto Ricans, who are thought to be Roman Catholic. From six a.m. to one p.m. on that inviting morning the two men kept count of all who passed. Twenty-nine people left the block: 1.5 per cent of the residents. The conclusion from this and from other surveys was clear: the overwhelming majority of people in East Harlem had no real relationship with any church, Protestant or Roman Catholic. ' Therefore,' wrote Benedict, ' we are without excuse.'

To a healthy sense of guilt was added a sense of dismay as they tramped East Harlem's streets and heard men's views on the church. Those to whom they spoke affirmed that of the three local forms of Christianity, all were irrelevant, and one was almost non-existent. They soon found out that this was true.

Benedict, Hargraves, and Webber visited fifty Pentecostal storefront churches most of which were wedged in between the gin mills and candy stores and tumble-down Chinese laundries. Here they often found a vital faith and a deep spirit of worship. Every evening twenty or thirty members would gather in each tiny church and find there a place of refuge and security. In their simplicity they were an easy target for sophisticated critics:

> Most of the churches . . . belong to the fringe world of
> Gospel-shouting revivalist sects that mushroom around
> the habitations of the poor, taking over storefronts or

undertakers' parlours with tinsel, a beat-up piano, and
variants of the motto ' Jesus Saves ' to offer the neighbours (for the price of a collection) a chance to chant and
dream for an hour or two of the Sweet Bye-and-Bye.
The Reporter.

In other words, they are to be dismissed as a mere escape
mechanism. But if any people anywhere need an escape
mechanism it is the people of East Harlem. Yet their religion
is more than an escape. The explorers discovered that many
of these churches had devout ministers who were proclaiming
what they believed to be the full Gospel of Christ. Moreover,
such men often proved their sincerity by giving their services
free of charge: the Church of the Living God, for example,
had a part-time pastor who supported himself with a janitor's
job in Manhattan. Further, many church members were
equally sincere, and expressed their devotion in a life of
prayer and in giving ten per cent of their gross income to their
church.

Yet East Harlem as a whole was unimpressed. Worse,
when it looked at the church notice boards, it was mildly
amused. *The Powerhouse Church of God in Christ, No. 2,
Inc.* was the name of one small church. *The Firstborn Church
of the Living God* was the name of another. And a notice on
the bulletin board of *The New Jerusalem Holiness Church of
the Lord Jesus* announced ' A Great Revival conducted by
the Holy Ghost through Elder Haynes and Mother Bent '.

But contempt was often stronger than amusement. The
pastors, for example, were almost always suspect, and the
question was invariably asked, ' What's he getting out of it?'
Usually, the answer was ' Nothing.' But not always. For
there were instances such as that of the Pentecostal minister
who drove in each evening from his apartment at the smart
end of town: sometimes he came in his Cadillac, sometimes
in one of his two other cars.

The services likewise failed to win respect, especially from
the youth of the district. The piano would play hymns to
catchy tunes, punctuated by the call ' Hands up, those who
feel better now.' The prayers would sometimes take the form
of speaking with tongues. The half-hour sermon would move
from one appeal to another: ' Who'll say " Amen "?' and the
Amens would come back. ' Who'll stand up for the Lord

tonight?" and some would stand up for the Lord. So far as most non-Pentecostals could see, worship was a matter of singing hymns to jazz tunes, of responding to calls to be born again, and especially of putting money in collection plates.

So these churches were rejected by the mass of men as utterly irrelevant to life. They did nothing to bring East Harlem's hostile camps together, for most of them ministered to just one ethnic group. Their worship often had no apparent effect on their members' lives: 'The thing I don't like about the Hallelujahs,' came the constant protest, 'is they talk against smoking and drinking in the church, and then go out and do it worse than anyone.' But their irrelevance was felt most sharply in their dominant concern to be 'separate from the world'. 'Otherworldliness' was right at the heart of the Pentecostals' faith. And most of East Harlem's residents held that if God wasn't interested in their world, in their plumbing, in their Welfare allowance, in their need for good police, if God wasn't interested in such earthly issues, then they just weren't interested in God—he was irrelevant. And very much to East Harlem's surprise, the three young men who were asking the questions emphatically agreed.

The second of the three local forms of Christianity was respected by some of the residents and dismissed by the vast majority. This was Roman Catholicism.

Its organisation was, of course, much superior to that of the Pentecostals. It concentrated most of its work in three well-attended churches ministering mainly to Puerto Ricans and Italians. It gave religious teaching in its ably-managed schools. It raised funds through its street processions, its carnivals, its gambling games. It attracted five per cent of residents to Mass on special Sundays. And despite the patient efforts of its priests, the general attitude towards it was one of indifference and even of lively opposition. 'The church?' said a middle-aged Italian, spitting on the sidewalk. 'The church? It's full of graft. All the priests do is try to get your money.' The point was not whether such convictions were true or false. The point was the convictions were there.

In a district like East Harlem which was disunited in everything except its opposition to the world of institutions, it was natural that men should suspect the sincerest endeavours of this church. It was so powerful. Its buildings—St. Lucy's, St. Cecilia's, Holy Agony—these were great symbols of a source of wealth and power which no resident possessed. It seemed that these structures must belong to someone else, to some other group, a powerful, wealthy group; and East Harlem had a bitter hatred for all such wealthy groups. 'What's the idea?' men asked. 'What're they after?'

To suspicion was added scorn at the apparent irrelevance of the Roman Catholic religion to the problems of everyday life. As with the Pentecostals, the church drew a line between the things of the spirit and the things of the world, and gave the things of the world second place. So most East Harlem men, with their overwhelming material burdens, could not feel that the church really cared for them as people. 'Why do we get so few men?' asked a priest at St. Lucy's in his morning sermon. '*Jesus* was a man. The twelve apostles were men. Nearly all the early Christian martyrs were men. But today . . .? Today, women come to church, and nice little girls with nice white veils. But men? Where are they?'

Some said that the men were so oppressed by problems of bread and drink and drugs that until the sacramental bread and wine were seen in sharp relevance to life that is lived on the city streets, those men would continue to reject the Mass as an ecclesiastical narcotic—and would seek fulfilment in more dangerous ways. 'I'm always rather dismayed,' said a local social worker, 'at the number of ex-altar boys who are addicts.'

It was perhaps no wonder that scorn and suspicion were matched by an unveiled cynicism at what most local men believed to be the utter irrelevance of the Roman Catholic church. If they had delved deeper they might well have changed their views. But they had no inclination to delve deeper. They were understandably content to sneer from afar; just as, for other reasons, they would certainly have sneered at the Protestant church, if there had been a Protestant church at which to sneer.

The Church Invisible: this was an almost exact description of the major Protestant churches in East Harlem. At least the Pentecostals and the Roman Catholics were *there*. But for the forty thousand inhabitants of the area mapped out by Don Benedict (99th to 106th Streets, and Lexington Avenue to East River Drive), a single Protestant church stood with its doors tight shut save for five hours a week. For good measure, a strong steel framework protected the doors themselves. It was an Italian Presbyterian mission church built to seat three hundred. Every Sunday morning about thirty individuals would gather for an hour in this place of worship where brass wall plaques recalled the days when it was a thriving, middle-class, ' respectable ' congregation. Now most of its original members had left the district, and this church, unlike so many others, had not closed down in order to chase after its clientèle. All the others had pulled out to middle-class neighbourhoods where, in such towns as Scarsdale, in nearby Westchester County, no less than sixteen of them ministered to the needs of sixteen thousand residents.

Instead of accepting responsibility for the community in a given area, the Protestant churches seemed fast bound to one class. ' There are churches that have moved six or seven times to keep up with their constituents,' protested David W. Barry, director of the New York City Mission Society. ' But does it befit the Church of Jesus Christ to go leap-frogging through the city after the families who intend to send their sons to Yale?' Certainly, some of them held on to a few working men, as though jealously maintaining representatives from the lower strata of society ; but most were content to preserve a situation which made Protestantism the most segregated institution in America. Instead of seeking out the lost sheep—whether black or white or speckled—they sought out those who thought as they thought, and dressed as they dressed, and talked as they talked. When this class moved from the district, the Church of God moved too.

So at a time when the working classes all over the world were moving into positions of power, and were gaining the conviction that they were the ' community of destiny,' the Protestant church was cutting itself off from them and neglecting the fact that the sign of the Kingdom is that the poor have the Gospel preached to them. So in East Harlem, as elsewhere in the labouring world, this church seemed to be a programme-centred structure which served the middle-classes, instead of a God-centred people who served the entire community. This was a picture of one more institution. It was not a picture of the church. Too often, however, the picture was correct; which meant that the church had betrayed its Lord. It meant that it had ceased to be the church.

So East Harlem's residents could choose between three forms of Christianity which seemed equally irrelevant. But the three observers saw that most of them just did not choose. They ignored the church. They continued to follow their own confused, fragmenting way of life, seeing no way out or round or through, but simply drifting hopelessly.

With this challenging conclusion, the friends went into action.

PART TWO

AN IDEA COMES ALIVE

5. BEGINNING IN THE BASEMENT

In a blinding snowstorm Benedict and Webber drove their old
Ford car through the Pennsylvania mountains, heading north
for Buck Hill Falls. It was January, 1948, and they had been
given ten minutes in which to put their plans before the
Division of Home Missions of the Federal (now National)
Council of Churches. Hargraves, at that stage, had other
commitments in New York, so the task of persuading the
national executives was in the hands of his two friends.

On arrival at Buck Hill Falls they made their way to the
conference room and took their seats, looking relaxed but
very determined. Benedict did most of the talking.

He had been a high school debater in Michigan where he
argued the case for socialism with such fire that his home
town American Legion post tried to get him expelled. But it
was not merely his fire which impressed the representatives of
the Council's twenty denominations; it was the overwhelming
evidence of painstaking research which emphasised, first, the
failure of the Protestant church in city slums; second, the
desperate longing of multitudes of slum dwellers for a faith,
' be it Christianity, Unionism, or Communism '; and third,
the immense enthusiasm of many divinity students to engage
in a city slum ministry.

The plan was for a three-man unit to work in East Harlem
for an initial period of three years. They would work as a
team on a total programme, but each would have direct
responsibility for a church. The three churches would lease
storefront structures, and the rental of each would be under
$100 a month. The ministers would live near the churches
and would begin their work by systematic calling, by giving
recreational leadership, and by co-operating with existing
community agencies such as settlements and welfare offices

and courts. As soon as sufficient interest was aroused, these activities would be followed up with worship services and Sunday Schools and participation in social action and in local politics. 'The churches' primary emphasis would be on religious life,' said Benedict, 'and at the same time the church would be the focal point around which life's problems could be attacked.'

The allotted ten minutes lengthened into an hour, for questions and answers came thick and fast. The session ended with Baptist, Congregationalist, Methodist, and Presbyterian representatives approving an eighteen-month trial of the plan and $10,200 to finance it.

A few months later Benedict and Webber were ordained in a Negro church in Harlem where they were charged with the care of churches yet to be born. Benedict and Hargraves (who was already ordained) were to give their full time to the work in East Harlem. Webber, who had been asked to become Assistant Dean of Students at Union Theological Seminary, was to divide his time equally between the project and the students, many of whom later chose to work in East Harlem.

On a hot August day in 1948 the team arrived in a lorry at a former butcher's shop on the corner of Third Avenue and East 102nd Street. Their first job was to convert the ground floor of the building into a storefront church. Waste water from a nearby tenement had been flooding the basement for years and was rotting the building off its foundations. They set to work, clearing the rubble off the trembling boards, and then began the task of prising up the floor itself in order to replace it with something stout enough to take the weight of a congregation.

When the first board was raised, an overpowering stench rose up and hit the workers, forcing a rapid retreat to the street. Investigation, with damp cloths tied tightly over nose and mouth, revealed an ancient barrel of rotting sauerkraut beneath the boards. When the men of the Sanitation Department came down the street, they flatly refused to go anywhere near the appalling smell, and soon the neighbours were treated to the unusual sight of three ministers in shirt-sleeves and dripping cloth masks, loading a huge crumbling barrel of foul sauerkraut on to a lorry, and driving off as fast as they dared, to dump it surreptitiously into the East River.

On their return a crowd of eager youngsters was waiting to watch developments. Benedict surveyed them with a grin and called on them to lend a hand, and in a moment a dozen teenagers were pulling up the rotting boards and loading them on to the truck.

Strong boards were salvaged from a razed building on the next block ; some were used to make a firm floor, and others were hammered together to make a rough cross and a communion table. By nightfall the store had begun to look like a place of worship. It was the first of the Parish storefront churches where Benedict and Hargraves were soon based as co-pastors, while two blocks away, on 100th Street, Webber and three students explored new territory in a persistent round of calling on people in their homes.

In the first few weeks the three men's early impressions of East Harlem as a chaotic society were multiplied a thousand times and they constantly met obstacles to their purpose which followed that of Christ and which they repeated every Sunday:

> The Spirit of the Lord is upon me,
> Because he hath anointed me
> To preach the Gospel to the poor.
> He hath sent me to heal the brokenhearted,
> To preach deliverance to the captives,
> And recovering of sight to the blind,
> To set at liberty those that are oppressed,
> To proclaim a year when men may find acceptance
>   with the Lord.

But they realised that if the church was to help bring wholeness to broken men, it had to exhibit that wholeness in its own life. That meant they had to start with themselves. They had to start by resisting the powerful pull towards fragmented living by displaying instead a community life which was unified by God and disciplined by the Gospel. They began by constituting themselves an interdependent group— a Group Ministry. The power of this Group Ministry was to lie in the fact that its members belonged to one another and depended on one another. Together the members determined on four disciplines to which they committed themselves.

First, there was the devotional discipline. Time was to be given each day to prayer and the use of common Bible readings. Every week the Group was to meet, and was to conclude its meeting with a service of Holy Communion. Every six months, three days were to be spent away from East Harlem, and used for quiet and conference and spiritual renewal. Included also in this discipline was the undertaking to have a visible centre of worship in the home: a cross, an open Bible, two candles, perhaps a painting.

Then there was the economic discipline under which the Group members were to be paid not according to qualifications but according to need, that is, according to the size of their families. In addition, there was to be a common fund: any money earned by speaking engagements or by writing was to be paid into this fund which would be used to meet special needs in the district.

The third discipline was vocational. This involved a commitment to their common calling to proclaim the Gospel in the city slums; it included the monthly submission of their work and their plans and their problems to the rest of the Group for criticism; and it called for an undertaking to make no change in their vocation without consulting the Group; and in the event of a change being made, to move only when a suitable replacement had been found.

Finally, there was the political discipline by which the members of the Group were to hammer out a position on all political and legislative issues affecting East Harlem, and then to work for that position, or else, if conscience would not allow, to hold their peace.

The disciplines were to bind the lives of the three men and their wives together in a covenant relationship which strengthened and sustained them in the face of East Harlem's tensions. The working out of the disciplines in their active ministry to the community slowly overcame the suspicions of their neighbours that the three were engaged on a project to study the people of the slums, or else were a part of a Communist racket to get control over the area. (' Why else should college graduates come and live in a place like East Harlem?') But the crucial importance of the disciplines lay in the fact that

they provided the framework for a common life which could
be observed by East Harlem, a life which was different from
that of their neighbours, a life which sought in all its aspects
to be subject to the Lordship of Christ. The four disciplines
were an essential element in helping men to see the Gospel as
well as to hear it.

The first worship service was preceded by a Sunday School
for children. Sixty boys and girls jammed themselves into the
tiny twenty-by-twenty foot room and they wanted to stay on
for the adult service. But it had already been decided that
while the church was to be a family church, its main concern
would be with adults, especially with men: and in any case
the place would seat no more than thirty-five grown people, so
the children had to leave in order to make room for their
elders.

All was ready for the service at eleven o'clock. The
ministers waited for fifteen minutes . . . for twenty minutes . . .
for a good half hour. Finally the congregation came—a vast
Puerto Rican woman with a great infectious laugh and with
what, at first sight, looked like a bundle of rags, but which, as
she reverently unwrapped them, flicking off cockroaches from
the folds, turned out to be a beautiful wooden crucifix. It was
a gift for the church.

So this first Protestant worship service began with the
hammering of a four-inch nail into the chapel wall and the
hanging of the symbol of what ' mission ' had meant to Christ.

' Let us worship God,' said Don Benedict. And the ministers, with their benefactor, bowed their heads in prayer.

Gradually, through patient calling, through contacts with the
children, and through the kind of social action which we shall
shortly picture, more and more men and women looked to the
little storefront church as to a gleam of hope in the dark.
There was Juan Ruiz, a Puerto Rican who had sung in first-
class opera ; there was George Livanos, a Greek dish-washer,
with Mary Lou, his gay Negro wife and their two small
children ; there was a young drug addict whom we shall call
Tony, desperately needing friendship (' I want you to take
time to listen to me, see? I want you to dig me, understand?') ; there was the teenager who had been arrested for

pandering at the age of eleven, and who had since been
investigated as a dope peddler on six occasions, and had
attempted suicide because ' There's just nothing left worth
living for.'

These, and many others, felt the pull of the rounded life of
the tiny church, and by the turn of the year (in January, 1949),
a second storefront was opened on 100th Street, with Bill
Webber as its pastor. And soon the Parish (that is, the two
young churches) was deeply involved not only in the district's
spiritual plight but also in its social chaos.

6. SOCIAL ACTION

It was the urgent practical needs of their neighbours that convinced the three pastors that despite the protests of local Pentecostal friends, they dare not spiritualise Christ's Gospel. They had good authority behind them. They remembered the early church, and how the Pentecost chapter in the Acts of the Apostles begins with a spiritual experience but culminates in an economic transformation: ' And all that believed . . . sold their possessions, and parted them to all men, as every man had need.' They remembered that God himself had expressed his love not only in spiritual terms but in terms of flesh and blood by coming right down to earth in the Person of Jesus Christ and meeting men's most material needs.

' And yet, the God of the churches which East Harlem knows,' wrote Hargraves, ' stays in celestial splendour far above this earth. But the God of this life is Vito Marcantonio [the near-Communist Congressman for East Harlem] and his Kingdom is the American Labour Party. Obviously the God who can get the plumbing fixed becomes the centre of faith for the great majority.' So far as the men of East Harlem could see, the church had no interest in the things that made up their life and no power to do anything about their problems, such as getting a job, or fixing up an apartment, or getting a less brutal police force. ' The church is all right for old women and kids,' they said. ' It's not for me.'

And of course the question was: Confronted with this attitude, what do you do? Do you preach that the Gospel transforms the whole of life, and do nothing about the dope pusher who is waiting for the service to end in order to hand out free heroin to the teenage choir? Do you proclaim a Saviour who came that men ' might have life, and have it more abundantly ', and do nothing whatever to help the man right there in the very front pew whose young son, Mario, is dying of tuberculosis? ' How,' asked Benedict, ' can we pray for Mario, and do nothing about the dismal slum in which he and a hundred other Marios are dying for the lack of good

clean air? Is that emasculated prayer anything short of
blasphemy?'

It was not that they wished to substitute material concerns
for spiritual ones. 'For God,' they insisted, 'the material *is*
spiritual—as spiritual as a babe in a manger, as bread and
wine, as the Body of Christ. Our sole concern is a religious
concern, and the social is an inseparable part of that religious
concern.'

Not that social action was easy or without its dangers. Those
who protested about poor sanitation stood a good chance of
being evicted. Those who reported drug racketeers might
very well be murdered. Residents had good reasons for keeping quiet, however grave anti-social activity might be. 'You
see a car pull up,' said an East Harlem mother, 'and they
push out a girl all beat up with her clothes torn. But the thing
you learn, the first thing you learn, is " I didn't see anything."
No matter where you were or what happened, you didn't see
anything.'

But slowly, very slowly, some parishioners began to take
courage from the example of the church.

In January, 1949, some residents discovered that their landlord had installed a thermostat near the furnace in the basement of his building. The automatic control was set for fifty
degrees, but that temperature was not maintained farther
than fifteen feet from the furnace. The landlord was using the
thermostat which the law demanded, a tremendous saving in
fuel was being made, and the families in the building were
freezing. They protested to the landlord and were threatened
with eviction. Then they turned to the Parish. They knew
that the Parish was concerned with souls. They also suspected
that it was concerned with men. Don Benedict led the tenants
to a nearby dime store where each of them bought a thermo-
meter. Through the next twenty-four hours they all kept
hourly readings and then presented their charts to a city
inspector. The landlord was taken to court ; he was fined and
warned that another offence would mean jail. The temperature in the building rose.

Through such events as these, residents began to understand what the ministers meant when they said in their sermons: 'We are here because we believe in the Lordship of

Christ over all things—and that means all economic things and all political things and all people.'

Many of those who were not reached by sermons were reached by Christian Action Newsletters pushed under the apartment door: 'Don't die from gas,' one such issue read when second-hand gas heaters were taking their winter toll of life. 'Have an inspector check your gas heater to see if it is safe. Sign this form and bring it to us.' And over the page, 'Fight T.B. with Christmas seals.' And again, 'Parish blood bank planned.'

Those residents who neither heard sermons nor read Newsletters began to see the church's concern for the whole of life in concrete action. They began to respond themselves.

The attack on 'airmail garbage' won immediate support. It was started by a white-haired twenty-nine-year-old divinity student who had joined the three pastors and who was living and working on 100th Street. This was Norm Eddy, a big man in body and spirit, who had seen extensive action with the American Field Service in the Middle East, North Africa, and Italy. He recruited five or six members of the church to tackle the problem of the garbage that was regularly tossed out of apartment windows and that littered the streets below. The small church group appeared one morning armed with long-handled brooms, and when they began to sweep their way through the block, they were joined by many other residents and cheered by all the onlookers as they advanced down the street, singing, to the tune of 'Roll Out the Barrel':

> Sweep, sweep East Harlem,
> We've got the dirt on the run;
> Sweep, sweep East Harlem,
> Our job has just now begun:
> Stop airmail garbage,
> Because it fouls up the air:
> Now's the time to use the ashcans,
> Because that's why they're there.

Soon after this a group of youngsters was formed into a gang whose members called themselves The Puritans. Led by a student worker, they began a clean-up campaign on an empty lot which had become a rubbish dump for the tenements which ringed it. They had not been at work an hour on a raw April morning before they were joined by many adult residents of the block. By nightfall eighty tons of rubbish had been removed in nineteen truckloads; the lot had been scraped as clean as a bone. It became an informal community playground: but first it served as a stage for an Easter pageant.

By mid-1949 the churches were in close contact with the many secular agencies in the district, and wherever possible they worked in close co-operation with them, handing on to them their detailed reports, and helping in such practical tasks as chest X-ray drives by the District Health Committee.

Co-operation was by no means always possible. The city's social workers tended of necessity to be overworked teams of experts who had to compartmentalise aspects of people's lives without seeing the over-all pattern and need. One agency dealt with school problems, another gave financial assistance, another dealt with delinquent youth, another with health, another with court cases. There was urgent need for someone to sit down and try to see a person's problem in relation to his life as a whole. And when the pastors tried to do this, they discovered that there were serious gaps in the existing services, and that these called for social action on a patient long-term basis.

One such gap was in the area of housing. The number of housing regulations and agencies and courts was staggering even to a person with professional training, let alone to an illiterate tenant with nowhere to turn for help. So the Parish established a Housing Clinic which was staffed by ministers, laymen, and lawyers: it was soon very much in demand.

Late one bitter November night a knock came on the door of the pastor in charge of the Clinic. It was Josh, a layman from 102nd Street church. He came with the news that a nearby apartment had been gutted by fire and that its occupants were homeless. 'We gotta help these guys,' he said. It was Saturday and 10.30 p.m. The pastor's sermon was unprepared. He was tired. But the family was practically penniless; it had nowhere to go; and the Housing Authority regretted that nothing could be done till Monday morning. The pastor rose from his desk, put on his coat, and went out with his friend. Before long another apartment had been found, and a church member who owned a truck had brought it to the scene of the fire. At midnight, Josh and another layman with two of the pastors were moving charred tables, boxes, and a weighty chest down three flights of stairs to the truck. They paused for breath on a landing where a neighbour had been watching. 'Why do you do this?' he asked. 'They're not members of your church. They're not members of any church. Why do you do it?' There was an answer. It had to do with the God who never said he loved the church, but who said he loved *the world*. When the job was done, the sermon had not even been begun. And yet perhaps it had already been preached.

But the approach to the housing problem covered much more than urgent crises. With military precision the Parish drew up its plans for Operation Tornado. This was a programme of 'education and action', and contained page after page of specific, detailed objectives:

To achieve improvement in housing conditions through prior lien law, tenant-landlord court, rat control legislation.

To gain acceptance for Puerto Rican and Negro families in non-urban Protestant communities where we already have contacts.

To co-ordinate movement of Puerto Ricans to rural areas on Displaced Person basis.

And on and on and on. It was 'a social action programme planned for a long stretch of time which can provide structure and meaning to our smaller social action efforts.' Survey after survey was undertaken: '3,000 homes were visited by 100 parishioners and 1,000 forms were secured which gave details of shocking conditions.' And again: 'In ten blocks over 1,200 violations of a major nature were found and turned in to the Department of Housing and Buildings.'

It was true that the Parish's enthusiastic plans often outran its strength and abilities. Schemes like Operation Tornado looked immensely impressive on paper and much less impressive in terms of what was actually achieved. And yet a great deal was achieved. And the extravagance of the plans was matched by an extravagance of unremitting work which undoubtedly played a real part in creating the present improvement in the housing picture.

Another gap in existing services was in the area of health. The city's large hospitals and efficient clinics were ready night and day to deal with major sickness and injury. But the family with the normal run of health problems did not fit easily into this structure. So a Medical Clinic was started. It had a full-time nurse, and a volunteer doctor who gave three afternoons and a morning a week to deal on a personal level with the sick of the Parish.

But the gap which no one seemed eager to fill was that which concerned the need to oppose police brutality. A few months after the work of the Parish began, a local teenager was shot in the back by a neighbourhood policeman. The tension in the district was acute, but 'What can you do against the cops?' Don Benedict headed a protest that wound up on the steps of the police station and led the crowd in prayers for the police. Instead of dispersing the demonstrators, the patrolmen stood silent throughout the intercession.

Many smiled at the naïveté of the action which in fact was no more amusing than the sight of Christ praying for Jerusalem. But action did not stop with this single demonstration. The Parish Minutes of staff meetings reflect the care with which the matter was pursued: 'Mark Lane [a local lawyer] reports severe case of police brutality at the station. Voted to get Christian Action behind it and have Archie serve as staff co-ordinator to gather facts and propose action.' 'Joe reported last night's case of his boys being picked up and beaten by the police. Norm will keep documented case histories.' It was this systematic accumulation of a mass of evidence which, as we shall see, finally got action from the Police Commissioner himself.

However, underlying most social problems was the inescapable disease of economic insecurity. When Norm Eddy became pastor of 100th Street, he approached this issue with characteristic patience. He writes:

We singled out eight men and women in their twenties,

and we asked them to pledge themselves to get together once a week for frank discussions of the problems which bothered them the most.

From the beginning it was made clear that the leaders had two ulterior motives. They wanted to confront the original eight, and any who joined them, with God and Jesus Christ. They also hoped by the fall of the year to have a group of people seriously discussing the basic economic problems of East Harlem and its citizens with a view to some form of action.

This group started meeting in one of the staff apartments. They called themselves the Christian Economics Group. Forty-five different individuals drifted in and out of the meetings during the first year. Of these, sixteen became regular. Within a matter of weeks a pattern evolved. The first hour was devoted to a frank, almost brutal, discussion of every conceivable problem on the minds of the group: race prejudice, attitudes towards parents, sex, rearing of children, dreams, psychology, ways of earning and spending money, ideas about religion. The second hour was devoted to a discussion of money and problems related to it. Gaining hope and enthusiasm, we soon introduced the idea of a credit union. By September, the entire group accepted a credit union as the goal towards which they were all working: in this union, members would pool at least a part of their savings, and loans would be granted to those who were in need or who wished to make improvements of a worthwhile kind. After the discussion of money and economics came the third integral part of the meeting: refreshments, informal talk, and the natural development of a social life within the group.

Free talk broke down unspoken prejudices. Self-education for leadership in an undertaking to help other people built mutual respect and the realistic hope that together we could face the problems of city living. All of this, followed by informal socialising, developed a solid friendship among the members of the group. It was from this friendship that all else grew.

Under the heading of ' all else ' were included 101 members of the East Harlem Protestant Parish Federal Credit Union.

Under the same heading came several people in the group who joined the church, and several more who took on responsibility although they had never before shown the slightest inclination to face East Harlem's problems. But much more than this was included, as Norm Eddy recounts:

A widow with three children to support took out a loan from the Credit Union. Sickness prevented her from working and from repaying her debt. When a member of the Board of Directors called on her, he did not go as a loan collector, but as a friend. When he discovered that she had other debts as well on which she was paying more interest, he showed her how she could take out one new, larger loan from the Credit Union, pay off all her debts with the money, and repay the one loan more slowly at a lower rate of interest. At first she was stunned into silence. For years no one had cared whether or not she made both ends meet. Now she saw hope. She took the chance.

Day by day, the Credit Union and its lay leaders are helping people to solve their own economic problems. It is their conviction that this is in keeping with the teachings of Jesus, who did not use the word ' love ' in the Lord's Prayer, but did show an interest in people getting enough to eat.

There were those who held that all this involvement in problems of garbage, housing, police, and poverty was consuming time which would have been better spent in preaching the Gospel. The Group believed that this *was* preaching the Gospel. And while they had behind them the whole Biblical tradition, they were especially fond of quoting St. James's protest that pure religion does not consist merely in keeping one's own hands clean, but that ' Pure religion and undefiled . . . is this: To visit the fatherless and widows in their affliction, and to keep himself unspotted from the world.' Social involvement *and* holiness. Set them apart, and religion is defiled. Unite them, and it is pure.

To neglect the social was to be more 'spiritual' than Jesus Christ had been. For, as Archie Hargraves argued, 'The proof Christ gave that he was God's Messiah was not only that the Gospel was preached to the poor, but first that the blind, the leper, and the lame were healed.' It was East Harlem's crying need for social healing that had compelled so many of its people to reject the church as irrelevant, for its preoccupation with 'the things of the spirit' seemed to sanctify the unjust world which they endured. In any case, the core of the Gospel was not that the Word became spirit, but that the Word became flesh. And this meant that the Gospel had to be expressed in very human terms, in terms of social action, in terms of flesh and blood. Words alone were not enough.

But neither were deeds. The Group saw very clearly that social action could be no more than valuable first-aid work which did not even begin to reach down into the roots of life. But the point of the Gospel was not just to patch up society's wounds ; it was also to grapple with the wills of the men who had inflicted those wounds, and who might well inflict them again. The Gospel had to get beneath the skin, it had to penetrate men's hearts and there renew the springs of life right where society begins. This meant evangelism. It meant the imperative necessity of preaching, because, as Webber expressed it, 'We begin to see that our first task in communicating the Gospel in East Harlem is not horizontal. It is vertical.' The horizontal issue was one between men and men. The vertical issue was one between God and men. And while both had to be pursued at the same time, the horizontal cancer could not be finally excised without the vertical gift of God's grace. There had to be an Advent. Sometimes it came in strange ways.

The Python Knights and the Latin Gents were preparing for a full-scale battle. There had been jealousy in these teen-age gangs over two sisters and it was to come to a head in a fight with knives and guns. Lonny and Josh were Latin Gents and also members of the church; that morning they brought the news to George Calvert, who was then a student working in 104th Street church, and who later became one of the Parish ministers. They hoped that he might help bring peace and prevent the near-certainty of killings.

That afternoon a few Python Knights appeared on 104th Street, and soon a knife battle broke out between them and a dozen Latin Gents. At the height of the fight one of the leaders of the Knights was stabbed right through his hand and left bleeding and in agony on the street, clutching his hand to his breast. No sooner had he been bundled into an ambulance than more gang members began to gather in the rival districts. They used lamp posts and telegraph poles for target practice. Their leaders sent runners to scour the district and call all their men to the battle. Two or three hundred of them began to gather. Except for the gangs the streets were cleared.

By now, George Calvert was at a bedside in Mount Sinai Hospital. He had done all he could to reconcile the enemies and now he knew that the time had come to speak the only word that ultimately mattered. Jackson, the wounded man, lay back, no longer in pain; and he listened in silence as his visitor spoke of the Cross, of forgiveness, of Christ. Then Calvert rose and left the ward.

It was not easy to round up the leaders of the gangs in such a tense situation, but Calvert was widely trusted, and by ten p.m. he had them in the hospital for a conference in a side room. Jackson came in and faced the other leaders. He was nursing his pierced hand. He saw the man who had stabbed him standing by the door. And when he spoke of forgiveness and of how Christians should live together, the rival groups listened intently and in absolute silence. ('Reach hither thy finger, and behold my hands'—Christ's words to Thomas kept beating into Calvert's mind.) 'If you fight it out with guns and knives,' said Jackson, 'you're taking the easy way out. The hard way is to forgive.' And there was reconciliation. At least for a time there was a truce: the Truce of Mount Sinai. But it was based not on Law but on the Gospel; on the Gospel of grace, of forgiveness, of Christ.

'Every activity,' read a Group Ministry report, 'and every

bit of casework should be thought of in the light of the question: How can we witness to the power of Jesus Christ in this situation?' They were convinced that a clear-cut evangelistic emphasis had to accompany social action because it alone could lift men's eyes from their ministers to their Maker and thus reshape society not in man's image but in God's.

This fundamental fact was underlined in a typical Group Ministry report which insisted: ' Evangelism is our total and only reason for being in East Harlem.'

This was true. But those who were understandably worried by the Group's emphasis on radical social involvement asked, ' What do they *mean* by evangelism? Just what *is* the Gospel, for them?' The surest answer to such a question came from those church members who for more than eighteen months had been learning from the Group what the Gospel was: people like Mrs. Mitzie Handy, for example.

Mitzie was overwhelmed when she was asked to be the preacher on Laymen's Sunday, 1950. Eventually she consented. ' After all,' she said, ' I am on the Church Council, and I guess I should be able to preach the Gospel. Just the same I'm scared.' This was her sermon:

For nearly two years I have been coming to this church. This morning I'd like to tell how I feel about coming and what the service means to me.

When I first became a member of this church I felt so proud. I was glad to find a church around the corner where I could come regularly. Away from the church for many years and finding myself lost in this big city, I was very happy to be able to come to this church. Going to this church was for me becoming a Christian. Since I became a Christian I find myself close to God. I think of him in my daily life and I seem to know him better.

All of us have things in our life during the week that make us feel far from God. It may only be that we are trying to get the children off to school in time. Maybe they are bad and won't do as they are told. I know I find myself very mad at times and curse at the children. When they are away at school I suddenly feel how wrong it was of me to do so, and I ask God to forgive me.

There are many things in our family life that make us forget what we are asked by God—to live as Christians and to love one another. With our neighbours, too, our relations are not what Jesus commanded. He said we are to love our neighbours as ourselves. But often we find ourselves not able to even get to know, never mind love one another. . . .

I think more than anything else that this is what coming to church Sunday means to me. The opportunity to start all over again. To come here and stand with you as we pray together. All the mistakes and anger of the week gone past fade away. What seems real to me is God himself and his forgiveness—I can begin another week anew.

Coming to church on Sunday is more than a habit. It is something I myself plan all week. It seems as exciting as a date. But it is not our coming to church that is important or how good we look in appearance but the gift that God gives us there. For God's gift each Sunday is of himself.

When we come to church we are like the woman who came to the well. We are met by someone we did not know before. Here in church he offers us a drink of water that will spring up into everlasting life. He also offers the water that can make us clean again and fit to be his worshippers. Here too he offers that drink that will strengthen us to do the work of another week.

For Mitzie Handy the Gospel was the miracle of forgiveness, 'the opportunity to start all over again'; it was also the gift of God's strength 'to do the work of another week'; and if we judge by the number of times she mentions it, the Gospel was supremely a matter of the reality of God himself: 'I find myself close to God. . . . I seem to know him better. What seems real to me is God. . . . God's gift is of himself.'

There was an increasing number of men and women like Mitzie Handy in whose lives the Gospel was taking root. Many, like her, were young, and able to express the reality of the Gospel in practical ways. ('I don't know, Mitzie,' said a Spanish neighbour, 'I've been here for three years, and you're

the only person who's spoken to me.' Some were old like
Miguel Rivera, and able to express the Gospel simply by what
they were.

Miguel was seventy and very nearly blind. He felt his way
along the streets with a broken stick and an outstretched
hand. His face was wrinkled and very kind ; somehow he
looked as though he'd known a lot of suffering. His pastor
had arranged to visit him one evening in his room in the
dingiest part of Madison Avenue. Miguel was out on the
sidewalk to greet him, and the minister felt refreshed just to
be with him. Slowly they climbed a few flights and felt their
way through the dark, stale stench of a mouldering building
to the room that was his home. The dark brown paper on the
dirty walls was peeling. The ceiling sagged. Three-fourths of
the space was taken up by his bed, and on this they sat down.
They talked a little. Mostly they just sat, at ease in one
another's company. Finally Miguel got out his Bible. Many
of the psalms he knew by heart ; his favourites were heavily
thumbed, and the pages were yellow and worn. They looked
at them one after the other, and the pastor saw that they had
one thing in common—they were all psalms of praise. Not
psalms of consolation for a man who lived in Manhattan's
greyest slum. Psalms of praise . . . The 95th was the most
thumbed of all: ' O come, let us sing unto the Lord: let us
come before his presence with thanksgiving.' ' And there I
always stop,' he said, paying no heed to the scratching of a
rat behind the wall. ' And I say, Alleluia ! Glory ! Alleluia ! '
His face might have been that of Christ transfigured on the
mount.

The growing church in East Harlem was convinced that it
had to work to banish rats from such apartments. It had to
do all it could to cleanse the society in which such men were
living. But altogether apart from the intrinsic splendour of
Miguel Rivera's life, the fact remained that the most potent
cleansing agents were lives like his in which God's glory
could be seen, lives which had what Jesus called ' the peace
of God '. This was not the peace of the graveyard ; it was the
peace of the living God without whom East Harlem's seething confusion would forever remain the same. And it was this
whole region of social chaos which was being undermined

when the Parish affirmed, 'Our essential aim is to confront men with the person of Jesus Christ.'

How was this aim pursued? How were men confronted with Christ? Mostly in humdrum, undramatic ways, but occasionally in ways designed to placard the Gospel before the eyes of the neighbourhood.

Half an hour before midnight on Christmas Eve, 1950, about thirty men and women left 100th Street church bearing lighted candles in their hands. There were plenty of people on the streets, and many bystanders watched the lights move up Second Avenue to the corner of 101st Street where another group lit their candles from those of their friends. On to the next corner where 102nd Street's members were waiting, and the dancing lights which herald Christ's coming grew as more and more of his people walked together through his city to 102nd Street church. Not all who entered bore candles. Bystanders had joined the procession and there were some who followed it into the church which glowed with the lights held by many disciples. The warm simplicity of the manger scene beside the Lord's table had meaning for all who were there; and somehow, everyone seemed to respond to the great proclamation, 'Emmanuel . . . God is with us!'

But of course the serious business of evangelism normally took place in less obvious ways than this. It took place, for example, as a result of ministers and laity tramping up countless tenement stairs, knocking on thousands of apartment doors, and talking with people in their homes. This often led to helping them sort out their everyday problems, and this in turn led some to the surprising discovery that the church really cared. Much more often than not, that is where the discovery ended; at least for the time. But occasionally it went further.

Sometimes such visiting led to Bible study groups being formed in different apartments. On occasion these were followed by a common meal, sometimes by Holy Communion. Now and then they were the means through which Christ confronted people; often they led them further on the road to God.

Above all, this patient, time-consuming visiting, this 'wasting time' with people, often made strong human friendships through which some lives slowly changed ; like that of a middle-aged Puerto Rican, who after three months' calling, finally told a Parish pastor, ' Since knowing you, it seems I'm coming to know God, too.' This first tentative expression of faith led him to organise a men's group in the church ; later it caused him to join the church by confession of faith ; later still it inspired him to support his tubercular mother whom he had neglected for years. And in this way a fragmented existence began to turn into a life.

It was the same with Luis Cortez. Luis came to East Harlem from Puerto Rico when he was just fifteen. He was a boy when he arrived. Within two weeks he was a man. ' I was just a bum,' he said, ' sleeping in empty cars on the street or else up on the roofs.' He met Hugh Hostetler, a square-jawed Mennonite pastor, who in 1949 had become the fourth full-time Group Ministry member. They met in a candy store and often spent time together on the street, ' talking about nothing at all '. One Saturday night, Luis got involved in a fight outside the Blue Heaven Bar. His opponent was armed with a long rusty kitchen knife, and as Luis ducked and fell on his knees, the knife was driven into his back. As he fell, he cried out, ' God!' ' That's how I prayed,' he says. ' I knew there was some kind of God.' Maybe he knew through his friendship with Hugh ; maybe not. In the hospital he kept on praying, and in time, to the doctor's surprise, he was dis-charged almost as fit as ever. Back in East Harlem he met Hugh Hostetler again. Slowly a straightforward friendship grew. In the end Luis had joined the church and was leading one of the liveliest church groups in New York City.

For every Luis, there were a thousand others. Or as one Group worker wrote, ' We have to understand that, of the ten cleansed, only one will return to give thanks, to be a Luis. Anyhow, this " return " is more God's business than ours. Meantime, there are guys whom you've just got to love be-cause Christ loves them, whom you've got to help because they need you, with whom you've got to stick around because Christ " sticks around " with them in the street and the candy store and the unlocked car at night ; and they won't under-stand and they won't be changed, but they will see a glimmer of hope from a guy who loved them for Christ's sake.' And the significant fact was this: that to the kind of person who

could write in this way, men seemed to come who were ready
for the Gospel; so that again and again the Parish workers
found they did not have to raise the Gospel issue with their
friends outside the church; it was taken out of their hands.
'Now it is the world which starts the conversation,' they
found themselves writing. 'Now the drug addict asks the
religious question, and the secular lawyer wants to come home
and talk about the meaning of the faith.'

Apart from these indefinable, unplanned friendships, the 'con-
frontation with Christ' came to many in the regular worship
of the church: on Sunday evenings, for example.

The loud-speaker in the candy store next to 100th Street
church would be blaring out popular rhythm. High school
girls would be clapping and dancing on the pavement as the
jukebox flung the tune the whole length of the street. A boy
in a new felt hat, carrying a walking stick, would prance a gay
imitation of the girls while his friends would whistle and
laugh. Everyone would be beating time, singing, laughing, as
the beat brought vitality to the street . . . But when the time
for youth worship came, many of the teenagers would be
there in the church. Some would be there because recreation
in the church hall that night was limited to those who had
been to evening worship and to the discussion which followed.
Most would be there because the worship was not stereotyped,
but tried to meet them just where they were.

At one youth service an expert musician with special
knowledge of jazz was the guest. During the singing time
before the service he sat at the piano, trying out different
rhythms. He asked, 'What is the text for tonight?' 'Seek,
and ye shall find,' came the answer, 'ask, and it shall be given
you; knock, and it shall be opened unto you.' He began to
line out a beat, humming, 'Seek, seek, seek.' Some of the
boys who usually stood outside or in the back during this
time came up and gathered round the piano and began to join
in. Before the service started one hundred young people
seated in the sanctuary of the church had worked out a swing
version of the text. Those who had been hardest to reach in
the past and most bored by many of the Sunday nights were
the most eager participants. As the worship leader wrote later,
'When the time came for the reading of the Scripture, some-

how these verses did not come out to the same ears that had heard them before. In a new way there was a listening, as if to say, " These are my words ; I know them ; they are part of me." '

If this had happened often, the church could easily have turned into a circus. It did not happen often. Dramatic variations in the regular form of worship were sometimes marvellously helpful in trumpeting the message of the Gospel. But normally the Good News of God was brought home to people in the steady, ongoing life of the church: especially through its Sunday morning worship.

8. STRONG PRAISE

As the worshippers assemble in the storefront church, a medley of familiar hymn tunes is being played as a quiet piano prelude. This is the first congregation which was formed three years ago, in 1948; its pastor is still Don Benedict, and he is helped by Carlos Rios, a member who has just become the church's Spanish-speaking lay pastor. Sunday morning at eleven o'clock is traditionally a time when East Harlem is in bed; but now in response to the living and the preaching of the Gospel about sixty people are gathering; Negroes, Puerto Ricans, men and women of European stock —they laugh and talk on the steps outside before entering the quiet of the church.

They take their place on the rough benches which seat four or five people each; some bow in prayer; some just sit, drinking in the peace of the place. The lighting is soft and the colours glow; the deep red of the high east wall, the golden brown of the cross upon it, the cream white of the communion table with its open Bible and its two unlighted candles.

As the prelude draws to a close, two teenagers each receive a lighted taper from the pastors, and then advance up the aisle. The congregation stands as they mount the three steps and as they light the candles, one of the grey-robed ministers, cries out from behind the people:

" The Lord is nigh unto all them that call upon him, to all that call upon him 'n truth. He will fulfil the desires of them that fear him; he also will hear their cry.'

The congregation is not looking at the minister, but straight ahead, at the cross; perhaps some remember the words at the top of their Service Sheet: 'We begin our worship with what *God* says to us.'

Then the pastor's voice again:'

' Let us praise God with Alleluias!'

And the whole congregation sings the threefold praise to the strong tune of Palestrina:

' *Alleluia! Alleluia! Alleluia!'*

'Let us invoke God's Holy Spirit,'
comes the bidding as heads are bowed.

'Eternal God who hath made us and given us life';
and back comes the response:

> *Thine is the kingdom and the power and the glory for ever and ever.*

'Eternal God who hath given us Thy Son Jesus Christ';

> *Thine is the kingdom and the power and the glory for ever and ever.*

'Eternal God who abideth with us in the Holy Spirit';
the Puerto Ricans are responding:

> *Tuyo es el Reino y el poder y la gloria por siempre jamas.*

'Eternal God who hath given us the promise of an ever-lasting kingdom of love';

> *Thine is the kingdom and the power and the glory for ever and ever.*

'Eternal God speaks to us in this hour, that we may rise up as eagles and proclaim thy justice throughout the earth';
and the final response of those who are learning how to rise and how to proclaim:

> *Thine is the kingdom and the power and the glory for ever and ever. Amen.*

During the singing of 'A Mighty Fortress is Our God' the two pastors walk forward with the choir members who are also robed in light grey gowns; they take their places in pulpit and choir stalls. The people enter vigorously into the spirit of the great German hymn:

> 'Did we in our own strength confide
> Our striving would be losing.
> Were not the right Man on our side
> The Man of God's own choosing.'

As the sound of the piano dies away, the pastors kneel before the cross and the people bow in their pews. There is a time of silence before they all unite in prayer:

'Most holy and merciful Father, we have done many wrongs, and have made many mistakes. We have followed too much our own wishes. Our hearts are not right. We have paid too little attention to the call of our consciences which try to put us straight. We have disobeyed thy holy commandments. We have not done those things which we ought to have done ; and we have done those things which we ought not to have done. And when we compare ourselves with thy Son Jesus Christ, there is no good in us.

' But thou, O Lord, have mercy upon us miserable sinners. Spare us as we confess our sins. Bring us back into thy family as we say we will strive to do better. And give us strength of mind, body, and purpose to do that which is right. Give us this pardon through Jesus Christ, our Lord, who was born and died for our sins. We ask it all with bowed heads and in his holy name. Amen.'

Then with a marvellous restraint the whole congregation slowly sings the *Kyrie*, the Cry for Mercy:

> ' Lord, have mercy upon us!
> Christ, have mercy upon us!
> Lord, have mercy upon us!'

And in the hush that follows, one of the pastors proclaims the fact of God's forgiveness . . . and then all repeat the Twenty-Third Psalm, an assurance of God's pardon and of his constant care:

> '. . . Surely goodness and mercy shall follow me all the days of my life: and I will dwell in the house of the Lord for ever.'

In the stillness there is a profound sense of what can only be called, quite simply, *reality*. Most of the people are looking away from themselves to the mercy and majesty and love of God ; they are being forgiven. This is a moment so spiritual (in a Christian sense) that its texture can almost be felt ; the forgiveness can almost be seen in the sanctuary ; one can almost get hold of it, almost grasp it in one's hands: the people of God are receiving what they most need to meet life's harsh demands ; slowly, and despite repeated failures, they are becoming the Household of God.

The prayers continue with Thanksgiving in English and in Spanish. Some of them come straight from the Book of Common Prayer: ' Almighty God, who hatest nothing that thou hast made . . .' (true ; but a bold affirmation for East Harlem) ; other prayers are extempore and are focused on events of the past week. When the Thanksgiving is over, there is a pause, after which the congregation sings the Lord's Prayer. Men and women of different races and languages, and totally different backgrounds, unite in:

' Our Father. . . .'

' *Nuestro Padre*. . . .'

As the pastor lifts the Bible from the table and offers a prayer for God's blessing on the reading, the door of the church swings open with a bang, and a young Puerto Rican walks jauntily down the aisle, greeting his friends with a familiar ' Hi!' before taking a seat near the front. No one thinks anything of the incident; it is not an interruption; it is just a young man coming to church; some come in quietly; some don't.

' Let us hear the Word of God. . . .'

The lesson is read in English, then in Spanish, and the congregation responds by singing—the singing has such warmth and texture—the Gloria:

' Glory be to the Father, and to the Son, and to the Holy Ghost;

As it was in the beginning, is now, and ever shall be; world without end. Amen.'

' Let us sing the hymn on page 16 of the hymn book: " Spirit of the living God, fall afresh on me."' And as the congregation sings, the pastors bow silently in prayer.

Then comes the sermon, first in English, then translated extempore into Spanish. ' The sermon,' the Service Sheet declares, ' helps us to understand the meaning of God's word as it was read in the Scripture lesson. As we think about God's word, and listen to the sermon, the meaning of the lesson is made clear to us so that we can apply it in our own lives.' All week the pastor has been trying to help bring peace between two rival gangs. Last night he got to bed at two a.m., and was wakened at six for yet another conference. There has been little time for sermon preparation. But the lesson came from the Parish lectionary which was the basis for the Group member's private prayers, and which was read at the Staff Communion Service this Sunday at eight a.m.: with that on the one hand and his deep involvement in East Harlem's needs on the other hand, he speaks to the people, in

a language that they understand, of the ways of God with
men:

'We read these loaded sentences in Isaiah 53 about God
sending a man who was to serve him and suffer for his
brothers. Well, here was that man in Jerusalem.

'The strange thing was that when they brought Jesus
out before the crowd all beaten up, with the thorns
sticking in his head and the blood streaking his face and
all the people mocking him—that *then* Pilate said, "Behold, *the man*!" But he was right. This was the perfect
man. This is what it meant to be a man.

'A real man is one who will serve his God and will serve
his neighbour, no matter what. He may be laughed at.
He'll certainly suffer. And he'll help turn this wilderness
of a world into the City of God. . . ."

The sermon over, the Bible is returned to the Lord's table,
while the congregation starts to sing the rhythmic spiritual:

> 'Tell me, how do you feel as you
>   Come out the wilderness,
>   Come out the wilderness,
>   Come out the wilderness.
> How do you feel as you
>   Come out the wilderness,
> Leanin' on the Lord?
>
> 'O, we're leanin' on the Lord
> O, we're leanin' on the Lord
> O, we're leanin' on the Lord
> Who died on Calvary.'

Some people sway to the rhythm as they sing; everyone
enters into the spirit of the words:

> 'O, we feel like a-shoutin' as we
>   Come out the wilderness
>   Come out the wilderness
>   Come out the wilderness.
> We feel like a-shoutin' as we
>   Come out the wilderness,
> Leanin' on the Lord. . . .'

As the sound of the spiritual dies away and the two deacons gather up the offering, there is silence, except for the soft playing of the piano. Here and there, change is given from the plate. . . . Finally, the deacons mount the steps to the communion table where the offering is received and held up before the cross while the congregation sings, 'Praise God from whom all blessings flow.' And then there is quiet throughout the church for the moment of Dedication.

As the pastor rises to his feet and turns to face the people, there is a hum of conversation. This is an informal time when visitors are greeted and announcements made and subjects for prayer are gathered. Seven or eight members of the congregation rise to their feet one after another, asking that special thanksgiving or intercession be made for them or for those they know. 'Let us pray,' says the pastor as he kneels before the table. There follow the particular prayers, and then general prayers of intercession, some of which are extempore:

'We pray for those who today will steal for the first time ; for those addicts who will use the needle for the first time . . .'

while another prayer is traditional, taken today from the Gallican Sacramentary:

'May he be pleased to grant his
servants here peace and harmony . . .
to the bereaved comfort,
to the workers an honest wage,
to the hungry food,
and clothing to the naked,
freedom and new life to the prisoners,
and a home to the homeless.'

The silence that follows is not broken but somehow it is deepened by the sung response:

'Hear our prayer, O Lord,
Hear our prayer, O Lord ;
Incline thine ear to us,
And grant us thy peace.'

The prayers are ended. The climax of the service has come. All stand and look towards the cross, the table, the open Bible. And thus they make confession of the faith that binds them together in a Body that transcends both race and language:

'I believe in God. . . ."

'*Creo en Dios. . . .*'

The pastors turn, and as the congregation sings, ' Blest be the tie that binds our hearts in Christian love . . .' they move slowly down through the little church with its glowing colours —cream, gold-brown, deep red—and they give ' the right hand of fellowship' to every person present. As they move on, the members of the congregation shake hands with their neighbours, with those in front and those behind, until, the hymn ended, the Benediction is asked from the open door which leads out to the street.

No moment in East Harlem is so quiet as this moment. Everyone stands silent. It is as though they are taking a deep breath before plunging back into the world; as though they are laying hold as firmly as they can on what they have received in this hour. They watch the two teenagers go forward to snuff out the candles and then return to their seats. Still they are silent . . .

A dog barks outside. The piano takes up the strong hymn of praise ' Now thank we all our God. . . .' And the people of God move out into the street, laughing and joking, talking endlessly . . .

PART THREE

CHURCH MILITANT

9. FRONTIER STRATEGY

Before the eighteen-month trial period for the project was over, the Parish had won the confidence of its supporting denominations who gave the Group Ministry complete freedom of action. Now in 1952 the original four supporting churches (Baptist, Congregational-Christian, Methodist, and Presbyterian U.S.A.) had been joined by the Reformed Church in America, the Evangelical United Brethren, the Mennonites, and the Evangelical and Reformed Church. Representatives from these denominations, together with others from Union Theological Seminary and the New York City Mission Society, constituted the Parish's Administrative Board. To simplify relationships, an executive of one of the churches was appointed adviser both to the Board and to the Group Ministry with the task of interpreting the one to the other. The Mission Society handled most financial matters for the Parish whose rising budget was being met by grants from the eight denominations as well as by gifts from many churches and individuals.

Bill Webber continued to divide his time between the Seminary and the Parish. It was mainly through him that more than five hundred students were to work part-time in East Harlem, and over twenty were to commit themselves to a long-term ministry there. Webber was able to refresh the life and thought of the Parish by bringing to it the fruits of his own academic work, and by introducing to it visiting church leaders—such as George MacLeod, D. T. Niles, and Lesslie Newbigin—who made their own distinctive contributions during Parish worship and retreats.

By the time the work had entered its fourth year (1952) a Parish-wide organisation had evolved. In the densely crowded rectangle between First and Third Avenues, and 100th and

106th Streets, four Parish churches were located, one on every other street (100th, 102nd, 104th, 106th).

In the heart of the narcotics district Norm Eddy was pastor of 100th Street church: he was a Congregationalist, and was to become the force behind the church's pioneer work with drug addicts. His wife, Peg, was also a Congregationalist minister, and she was to emerge as a leader in the drive for better schooling in East Harlem. The Eddys' home, on the second floor of a dilapidated tenement, was becoming an oasis of sympathy and strength for hundreds of their neighbours.

Eddy had taken over 100th Street church from Archie Hargraves in June, 1951, when Hargraves, with the full support of the Group, had responded to an invitation to start similar work in a multi-racial district of Chicago. Already the seed which had been sown in the concrete of East Harlem was being scattered a thousand miles to the west, as it was to be scattered later in other cities, too.

Two blocks north of the Eddys, on 102nd Street, Hugh Hostetler had been pastor of the congregation for a year. A vigorous figure with a lively sense of humour, he had worked for two years in Puerto Rico, and his fluent Spanish was already opening many doors to the church.

Another two blocks north, on 104th Street, Don Benedict, with the original Parish congregation, had moved to a third storefront. He was joined by John Crist of the Reformed Church—a small, quiet graduate of Union Theological Seminary with great gifts as pastor and musician. Puerto Ricans were especially numerous near this church, and the talents of Carlos Rios—who had been a labour organiser in San Juan—were invaluable. It was his boundless enthusiasm for the vigorous life of the Parish that had made Carlos accept the job of lay pastor. He was always available for people ; so far as he was concerned, meetings of any kind always had to take second place: if it was a choice between filling in a health form for a visitor who had hours to spare and preparing the sermon for a communion service which was to start in thirty minutes' time, Carlos would always choose the health form. ' If you want a man to help you in an impossible fix,' read a leading article in the local Spanish newspaper, ' go to Mr. Rios in the church on 104th Street.'

The fourth Parish church was on 106th Street. Unlike the others, it was not a storefront. Church of the Ascension was the one regular Protestant church which the Group had found in the area; it was a plaster Romanesque brick building belonging to the Presbyterians. The congregation consisted of a bare handful of members, and when in 1952 it had been without a pastor for a year, the Presbytery appointed a minister and agreed to the church's joining the Parish: it remained part of the New York Presbytery and stayed Presbyterian in doctrine and life, and at the same time it was fully part of the Parish with responsibility to the Parish Board. Its new pastor, George Todd, was a graduate of Yale Divinity School. He was a quiet man with a natural warmth and self-composure; when working in the church he sat at a desk right beside the front door so that he was accessible to all who passed by; his home was just round the corner, up five tenement flights to a small apartment which had modern lighting, shelves of books, and a Rouault print depicting Christ on the Cross. In his spare time at theological college Todd had directed a radio programme which tried to give a Christian interpretation of the week's newspaper headlines: now he was seeking to interpret Christ to a district which often supplied the material for the headlines.

'What church do the people join?' was a common question asked by visitors. Those who joined the Church of the Ascension became members of the Presbyterian Church in the U.S.A. and also members of the East Harlem Protestant Parish. Those who joined one of the other three congregations became members of that particular interdenominational church in just the same way as those who joined a community church elsewhere became members of that particular interdenominational church: as with the members of Ascension, however, they were also members of the East Harlem Protestant Parish. By this time (1952), communicant members of the Parish numbered about 160; but hundreds more took an active part in the church's programme of recreation, social action, and worship.

Parishioners walking down 104th Street would sometimes pause at the window of what had lately been a Chinese laundry: now the Parish had its office there. Beyond a notice which asked 'May we help?' the passer-by would see Miss Florence Borgmann, the Parish administrator, dealing with piles of correspondence. Flossie, as she is known to multitudes of residents, had been for six years secretary to the chairman of a big industrial concern, had worked her way through college, and spent a year at Yale Divinity School before coming to work with the new East Harlem church 'to do children's religious education (so I thought!) . . . but in fact to find the staff ready for me with a miserable storefront in which they said "administrate"!' Maybe those who paused at her office window would have a son who was going to jail; maybe they would have landlord trouble; maybe there would be illness in the family; in any event, they would often go inside to share their tensions, to get advice, or sometimes just to pass the time. Flossie's problem was that she was a first-class administrator and also the kind of person to whom all and sundry would quite naturally take their problems. This meant that she spent most of the day in pastoral counselling and a good part of the night catching up on office work in the small apartment which she shared with another Group member. Those parishioners who came into the office might be referred to the Parish medical clinic where a doctor was in regular attendance and a Group Ministry member was a full-time nurse. Others might be referred for help to one of the Parish pastors or to a sympathetic lawyer who gave his services free three nights a week. Teenagers might be put in touch with one of the two street clubs which had rooms in two other Parish storefronts. Many would not be referred at all: they would find the answer in the office.

By the summer of 1952 many families were escaping briefly from the din and dirt of the city to the recently acquired church farm in the rugged country of Putnam Valley, New York. The farm was becoming a place for regular one-day outings for up to one hundred and fifty people at a time. An old school bus, which the Parish had bought, left 102nd Street about ten on Saturday mornings; ninety minutes later it was gasping its way up the steep hill to the ramshackle farmhouse, and soon afterwards its passengers (and others who had travelled in one or more of the four Parish station-wagons) were enjoying a picnic lunch on the grass in the quiet of the countryside. After lunch there was recreation for those who wanted it, but many were content to go picking berries, or to sit, talking and laughing in groups. When the evening meal was over, the outing closed with a service in the lovely outdoor chapel, and then everyone boarded the bus and the station-wagons, and turned their backs on the grass and the space and the wide sweep of the sky.

Some families—members of the Parish and non-members—were having the first holiday of their lives at ' Parish Acres ', as the farm had been called. Every week in the summer five or six families were there enjoying hikes, athletics, relaxation, and crafts such as making wooden crosses for their homes. Group Ministry families took turns in spending a week on the farm where counselling and serious discussion were more possible than amid the rush and distraction of the city.

The farm was also becoming a place of refuge. There was the drug addict, just released from jail or hospital, who needed to be out of reach of the dope pusher on the street; there was the young man who had just become a Christian, and who had to decide if this must involve him in a break with the gang of racketeers for whom he worked. Much more often there was the wife or the husband or the couple who had reached breaking point under the pitiless pressures of the city; in the quiet of the farm, and with the help of good companions, some were renewed and strengthened and enabled to carry on. But first of all, the farm was a place of retreat. The Group Ministry now held a one-day retreat there every month: they left East Harlem in the station-wagons on a Sunday evening and were back by the late afternoon of Monday, having spent their time mostly in worship and recreation and discussion (' Far too much discussion,' they frequently said). The farm was also a place of retreat for groups of lay men and women who got away to discuss the church's problems and opportunities, to make their plans, to draw up programmes, and to pray together.

' The farm is heaven,' declared a Councilman, ' undiluted heaven!' At all events, it was a precious mountaintop which brought men nearer heaven-on-earth. For most it was a mount of friendship where their lives were intertwined with those of others; for many it was a Mount of Olives where prayer and great decisions were made; and for some it was a mount of transfiguration where life began anew.

Through the worship and the rounded life of the four congregations, through the ministry of the medical clinic, the office, and the farm, the Parish was building a strong community which was reaching out creatively into the life of the whole district, including its political life.

10. POLITICS

Most thoughtful observers were right behind the Parish in its
programme of social action. But some drew the line when
they heard the Group say (as Don Benedict had said to the
Home Missions Council), 'The church must not be afraid to
participate in *political* pressure in order to bring about
change.'

The doubts were understandable. Engagement in politics
would put the church in such an ambiguous position. It
would inevitably bring misunderstanding. It would alienate
all those who claimed, 'The church must be above politics.'
But what do you do when the Congressman who is supposed
to be representing the interests of exploited men and women
on 104th Street secludes himself in his 86th Street office and
disregards their needs? 'He failed to vote,' reads a Parish
memo, 'on key public housing bills, voted against hospital
construction, voted against bills aiding education.'

What do you do when you know that three of the most
acute problems for all your parishioners are housing, hospitals, and education? Or to be more concrete: In East
Harlem rents were ten to fifty-eight per cent higher than elsewhere in the city. Between twenty-five and fifty per cent of a
family's income had to be spent on housing, and often condemned housing at that. This was blatant exploitation, and it
sometimes meant that sufficient money was not left over for
food and clothing and medicines. It meant that families were
hungry and cold and lacking medical care. The way to change
all this was a political way. And the Group had the uncom-
fortable conviction that if they neglected the political realm
they would not be able to silence a familiar voice: 'I was
hungry and you gave me no food, naked and you did not
clothe me, sick and you did not visit me.'

A tragedy on 104th Street made this conclusion inescapable.
An old man was struck down by a coal lorry that was trying
to beat the signal lights. Don Benedict saw the accident. His
first impulse was to pick up the bleeding man, put him in a

cab and drive at once to the hospital. That would have made
him literally a Good Samaritan. But he knew that such action
was illegal. The law stated that injured people might not be
removed. The only thing to do was to try to make him comfortable, to call an ambulance, and to keep the crowd back.
Fifteen minutes went by. Thirty minutes passed. When an
hour had gone the man had ceased to moan. After an hour
and thirty-seven minutes the ambulance arrived. The man
died on the way to hospital.

What was the church to do? The Group re-read the Good
Samaritan story and could not escape the fact that they had
to do something about men dying by the roadside: either that
or abandon their ministry. Christ's command seemed perfectly plain: If the law forbade their helping injured men
directly, and if medical aid took ninety-seven minutes to
arrive, then those who would not ignore his call had to do all
they could to ensure that aid came faster. And that meant
politics. It meant, in fact, a sound knowledge of political
structures, and a great deal of sustained effort in putting the
kind of pressure on the city authorities that would result in
men's wounds being bound up in time to save their lives. It
meant that to be a Good Samaritan *necessitated* being actively
involved in politics.

The Group argued in this way: It is clearly the will of
God that doctors be sent to the Jericho roads of this world to
patch up the wounded who have fallen among thieves. But
men would not be wounded at all on those roads if the police
were effectively protecting them from thieves: and the way to
better police protection is a political way. The question was
this: Does God approve his church's tending the ugly wounds
of the world, and deny his blessing to those who would prevent there being any wounds to tend?

The church was confronted with so many men—and
women and children—who had, as it were, fallen among
thieves, that its members knew they had to do everything they
could not merely to ease the pain of the fall but also to stop
the work of the thieves. It was not enough merely to appeal
to generous churches for funds to bring soup and clothes to
hungry men in cold apartments: the root of the problems
would remain untouched. And while Christ was most certainly concerned to relieve the immediate needs of his people,

he was even more concerned to prevent those needs arising again. The problems of hunger and clothes and rents might be problems of original sin ; but concretely they were problems of unfair wages, of exploitation by landlords, of inadequate rent legislation: that is to say, they were problems of politics. So the Parish became convinced that obedience to Christ must involve it in a fight for minimum wages, for relief, for un-segregated housing, for rent control ; and this, as one of the pastors put it, was a fight ' which can not be carried on suc-cessfully unless one talks politics with Congressmen, State Assemblymen, City Councilmen, and local political leaders— and preferably does political business with them.'

Failure to participate in this way was to abandon the political realm to wholesale secularisation. When Don Benedict ran for City Council membership in 1953, Carlos Rios was out on the streets seeking votes. He met a coloured Pentecostal minister who had a small church on 100th Street, and he urged him to persuade his flock to vote for Benedict.

' If he's a man of God he'll win,' came the reply.

' But doesn't God want our aid in helping him to win?'

' If he's a man of God he'll win.'

' But God doesn't pull down the levers in the voting booths!' protested an exasperated Carlos.

Back came the imperturbable reply,

' If he's a man of God he'll win.'

The man of God failed to win—as many men of God have seemed to fail. Perhaps he would have won with a few more votes from the Christian community. As it was, he failed, and men of goodwill on the City Council lost a creative Christian voice.

Political neutrality was impossible. To be politically in-active was to take a firm line against those whose urgent needs demanded political change. It was to sit back at ease in Zion while (by all human calculations) exploited men and women went to hell. To present East Harlem's addicts with a Gospel which taught that Christ redeems souls but not politics was not just to be profoundly unscriptural ; it was to present them with another form of dope. In fact, it was to sanctify a social order which, according to the Group, was ' rotten from its pimps to its police '.

To be concrete: How could the police be improved? On Christmas Eve 1953 a church member reported that an officer had chosen $50 worth of gramophone records from her store, and when asked for the money, had replied, 'Do you want protection or don't you?' A month later, a twenty-year-old youth was shot dead on 103rd Street. 'He was shot by a cop,' said a Negro minister. 'Why? Because he wouldn't give a $2 bribe to him. That's why.' Such incidents involved real people. They brought economic and personal tragedy. There was no redress save through politics. To do nothing to prevent their recurrence was to pass by on the other side. It was to enter the ranks of those whom Christ describes (in Matthew's alarming chapter twenty-five) not as mistaken, nor as misled, but quite simply as damned.

It was therefore as a matter of Christian obedience that the Group was forced to formulate a political philosophy:

First: Neutrality in politics is a myth. He that is not against the majority is for it. He is a reed bent in whatever direction the prevailing political wind is blowing.

Second: God is not only concerned with the soul of man but with the whole of man. He wills a just social order. His followers are therefore obliged to participate actively in seeking social justice. This means political involvement.

Third: Political institutions are sinful. So are all human institutions (including, incidentally, the East Harlem Protestant Parish). The Gospel cannot be equated with any political choice. Political parties will not bring about the kingdom of God. Sin is overcome not by us but by God.

Last: In short, we are worldly pessimists, but divine optimists. Our political motivation comes not from the faith that we are thus going to bring about a new world. We are confident only that it is God's will that we should work through all means possible, including political parties . . . to cast off oppression and to seek justice for all.

This philosophy demanded hard work and organisation. It meant that while no more than five per cent of total staff time was spent on active political affairs, yet the staff had to use

every moment of that five per cent, not only at election time
but the whole year round. It involved the Group Ministry in
a political discipline whereby they pledged themselves to act
as a group in studying legislative issues and in supporting
political parties and candidates; all members agreed to abide
by majority decisions or else to hold their peace. It involved
a full-time minister being given the duty, among others, of
keeping the Group informed on every item of legislation
affecting East Harlem as it came up on all levels. It involved
the preaching of political responsibility (not of political candidates) from the pulpit. And it involved the organisation of
each of the Parish election districts under a Captain who in
his spare time kept records of registered voters, encouraged
non-voters to register their names, and maintained card files
and calling lists ready for action when the time for a campaign came.

In these election districts a solid corps of people was sought
out and banded together; some were Group Ministry members, some were Parish church members, others were members of no church at all. Sometimes, for obscure reasons, the
efforts of this corps evaporated almost before they had begun.
At other times the members of the team took up their duties
with resolute efficiency:

> Begin to lay groundwork for campaign against Donovan
> as Democratic nominee. Centre lectionary, worship,
> Bible study and youth programme on ' The City ; the sign
> of man's evil and the sign of God's perfecting of his
> people.'

This Parish Council Minute was prepared before the 1954
political campaign. Behind it lay an attitude which was of
first importance: it was an attitude of worship. In opposing
Congressman Donovan's nomination in that particular primary election, the Parish did not first get in touch with the
Democratic party organisation. The first thing they did was
to worship God. Their primary concern was prayer and study
and praise in the context of God's love for the city. This
was not in order to give a religious flavour to their political
involvement; nor was it to seek God's blessing on plans
already made. The object was to see the political situation
from the divine perspective, and so to seek direction for their
involvement: direction from God.

Opposition to the inactive Donovan, and support for the Liberal Democrat Casper Citron, meant a fight against some of the most firmly entrenched Tammany clubs (the local Democratic Party organisation); for example, it was reported that in the club nearest the Parish office, over three hundred persons were beholden to it for their jobs; and such a number, with their friends and relatives, represented a powerful political machine on election day.

One of the Parish ministers served as leader of the Citron forces in East Harlem. A church member became full-time organiser of a Citron club in the local assembly districts. The entire Group and many church members worked hard to get the petitions signed, to make Citron known to all registered Democratic parishioners, and to get them to come to the polls and vote for him. On primary day this team manned all the election districts with runners to get the voters out, and with poll watchers to check on unfair tactics.

Citron won in the district manned by the Parish (he got ninety-six per cent of the vote on 100th Street). He lost the campaign as a whole by 760 out of 10,000 votes. This failure was important; but, as was proved later, on a long-term view the failure was not so much the point. For the first time in many years a high proportion of voters appeared at the polls in the party primary. For the first time in years the Tammany clubs had been challenged. For the first time East Harlem saw real hope of overcoming what many believed to be a corrupt political machine. For the first time there was a question mark in the minds of the men who had often said, ' If you want to get things done you don't turn religious; you turn political.' And one of the laymen who was taking a lead in church affairs had his own answer to a church member's protest, ' Politics is a dirty game: we Christians must keep out of it.' The answer was, ' Politics is certainly a dirty game: we Christians must get into it and help do away with the dirt.'

11. LOCAL LEADERS

It was not surprising that when visitors asked the pastors, 'What has the Group Ministry achieved in the last five years?' their invariable answer was, 'Nothing! But the church has achieved quite a lot'; for, increasingly, lay men and women were taking the initiative in politics, evangelism, the conduct of worship, and social action.

So the members of the Group stressed their conviction that they were dependent on the laity, and the laity were dependent on them; the church, they insisted, was an organism, a body—the Body of Christ—with a great many interdependent members, each bringing his own special gift to enrich the life of the church as a whole. 'The church is not a bunch of independent individuals,' they would insist; 'the church is a community of people who have pooled the different talents God has given them, so that in their community life they may express the different aspects of the love of God and may work together in the world as Christ's Body, as his representative.'

This belief was deeply and passionately held by every member of the Group. They went about their work expecting to find men and women with great gifts to offer, and they were not disappointed, for their parishioners went beyond St. Paul's list of gifts—teaching, prophecy, administration, service—by adding many others, including the gift of gaiety.

The first Parish wedding in 106th Street church was followed by a reception in the hall. The one hundred guests sat down at the tables and enjoyed their potato salad and apple pie and coffee. But after twenty minutes of quiet conversation the volatile Mrs. Rosa Valez decided that the party was moving too slowly.

To everyone's amazement she pierced two white paper plates with bright red plastic forks, and fastened the creation in her long black hair. Then, in her scarlet dress, the heavyweight Bible Class leader climbed up on to the trembling table and, amid gales of laughter, scattered the salt and sugar and empty plates with an improvised dance whose leaps and spins nearly brought the table crashing down on the knees of the helpless guests.

The gifts of lay men and women were finding expression in many other ways, especially in service to the community. In 1953 the seven-month-old daughter of a Roman Catholic woman on 103rd Street had been taken seriously ill. It seemed that the child had a defective heart. If her life was to be saved, there had to be an operation on the heart itself, and for this the doctors needed two pints of blood from fifteen people ; and they needed it within two days. Moreover, the blood had to be not just of one type but exactly the same in all respects. 'They say this will mean testing blood from hundreds of people,' the mother said hopelessly to her next-door neighbour, 'and how can I find hundreds of people to offer us their blood?' The next-door neighbour was Bill Cooper, youth group leader at 104th Street church. Among his gifts was that of administration, and he exercised it then without delay. He left his family to get on with their break-fast, and went out at once to recruit the nearest members of his church. That Saturday morning they offered their own blood, and then went knocking on their neighbours' doors, appealing for type 'O' donors for the rest of that long day. The hospital was fifty minutes away by bus ; it was an awk-ward place to get to and involved three changes. But before long, Bill Cooper's neighbours—Negroes, Whites, Jews, Puerto Ricans, Roman Catholics, Protestants—were queuing up at the hospital laboratory, having their blood checked, and dis-cussing the baby (and, from time to time, the man) who had drawn them all together. The baby lived. And East Harlem learned a little more about a church that was beginning to inspire lay leadership in many aspects of its life.

It was because of this fact that in the pastors' reports to their Administrative Board, the word 'Parish' (meaning the four congregations) was replacing the word 'Group', for the focus of church life was moving from the Group Ministry to the Parish as a whole, and laity and pastors were sharing much of the leadership through a simple administrative structure.

On the periphery of the Parish organisation were many activities which were open to non-members ; these were the means by which many residents reached the stage of wanting to join the church. After a ten-week period of instruction, a candidate for membership could join any one of the churches on public profession of his faith in Jesus Christ. The governing body of the church which he joined was called the Church Council, and with the exception of its minister members, it was elected by the congregation: this Council controlled all aspects of congregational life apart from such issues as the employment of pastors and of other staff, issues which few lay members yet felt competent to decide. The members of each Church Council and all Group Ministry members constituted the Parish Council: this Council made all decisions affecting Parish-wide concerns, with the exception of major policy matters, such as the use of funds, which at this stage were dealt with by the Group. Technically, the Parish Council was responsible to the Parish's Administrative Board (which consisted mainly of a representative from each of the eight supporting denominations): the Chairman of the Parish Council—who might be a minister or a lay man or woman—was always a member of the Board. So apart from certain areas which the Group alone controlled, authority in the Parish began with the local congregations who elected their own Church Councils; together the four Church Councils constituted the Parish Council, and that Council was represented by its Chairman on the Parish Administrative Board.

This organisation comes to life in the experiences of a young ex-serviceman and a gifted middle-aged woman.

George Calvert—working now (by 1953) as student pastor with Don Benedict—was sweeping up the litter on the vacant lot where 104th Street church had been holding its July Fourth festival. He had noticed the big Negro, in brown sweater and army slacks, who was watching the races and the boxing tournaments, and when Calvert asked if he would help, he smiled and seemed glad to lend a hand. A natural friendship sprang up between the pastor and twenty-three-year-old Sam Rogers; and within a week the young ex-serviceman was attending his first meeting of The Squad.

The Squad was a church club which was open to any young man who cared to come: there were about twenty members who enjoyed outings and basketball and games of snooker, and who came once a week to the formal Squad meeting.

Half the time at the meeting was given to frank discussion of such questions as sex, alcohol, narcotics, getting jobs; the rest of the evening was devoted to Bible study which sometimes seemed a complete waste of time, sometimes led to tremendous verbal battles, and occasionally confronted the members with the very heart of the Gospel.

Sam had never been keen on finding a job, and so he had time to be in and out of the Calvert apartment increasingly; soon he was attending Sunday worship at the church. Six months after the July Fourth festival, he asked if he might join the membership class so that he might join the church that Easter.

For ten weeks he attended the classes which followed the six pledges in the Parish Covenant:

1. To accept Christ as Lord and Saviour;
2. To meet regularly for counsel with a minister;
3. To be active in a nonchurch community organisation;
4. To plan church action each month for community goals;
5. To pray and read the Bible daily;
6. To 'walk together in love for God and for our neighbours'.

Sam learned that while church membership was impossible without acceptance of Christ as Lord, the remaining five pledges in the Covenant could be accepted simply as an ideal at which to aim. But when the time came for him to be examined, he had become sufficiently serious to see that it was the first pledge that stood between him and membership.

The four laymen who comprised the congregation's Church Life Committee sat with Sam beside the communion table in the little storefront church. It was their task to interview all candidates for membership, and as they talked with the grave young ex-serviceman about Christ and the Gospel, it became even clearer to him that he was faced with a choice between two ways of life. The discussion came to an end only after an hour and a half, and then the committee's chairman brought the news to George Calvert that the candidate felt he was not yet ready to join.

The next week Sam joined The Brotherhood. This was a group of older men which, like The Squad, was open to any who cared to come. Its members met weekly in their homes, and they had three objectives. First, they studied the Bible together. Second, they fought social evils by such means as listing a hundred heating violations by three local landlords and getting action from the City Department of Buildings. Third, they prayed together at the end of their weekly meetings, each man praying round the circle before the benediction was asked.

It was after his third meeting with The Brotherhood that Sam stopped living on unemployment insurance and got work as a factory hand. As the months went by he was taking more and more responsibility, and soon he was asked to join a committee of church members and non-members which was trying to give friendship and help to local drug addicts.

Six months later he attended a Brotherhood retreat at the Parish farm. The theme of the retreat was 'How can a man be a Christian in East Harlem?' None of those present was more concerned than Sam to improve conditions in East Harlem. None was more conscious of the fact that without God's help nothing fundamental could be done. The retreat closed with a resolve to pray and work more closely together, and with the election of Sam Rogers as President of The Brotherhood.

Two months later, at one of his regular meetings with Calvert, he was ready to take the first pledge in the Parish Covenant. He met the members of the Church Life Committee who approved his admission to church membership. And on the next Communion Sunday he knelt at the Lord's table with the hands of the ministers and Councilmen on his head, while prayer was offered for one more man who had confessed his faith in Christ and who was about to receive the bread and wine which symbolised a new allegiance that governed the whole of life.

Carmen Martinez' story is typical in quite a different way.

Carmen is a slender woman of medium height, with black hair and kindly eyes and a gift for conveying the impression that the old green dress which she invariably wears has just come off the rack in Lizzie's Market. She had been disillusioned with the church and gave up her membership long before she left Puerto Rico to arrive in New York City with her two small children in the winter of 1950.

It had been warm in Puerto Rico, but her East Harlem apartment was nine degrees below freezing at midday because the tenement boiler was broken and the landlord refused to repair it. Carmen's halting English and her ignorance of city ways gave her a sense of utter helplessness. She called on her next-door neighbour, who was a Parish member, and learned to her surprise that ' the minister is having a stand-up fight with the folks in the Housing Authority.' Soon Benedict arrived with the news that after an hour of argument and threats, the Authority had given him the keys to twelve vacant apartments in a nearby tenement—with heat. Fifteen minutes later, with the pastor's help, Carmen Martinez and her children had made their first real home in East Harlem.

A year later, when she was forty-one, her uncle was shot dead in a gang fight over on the west side of the city. Carmen was his only relative, and was responsible for all the complicated legal details. She had already decided to turn to the church for help when the Parish's lay pastor, Carlos Rios, knocked on her door. Together they went through the long-drawn-out formalities at the mortuary, the Police Department, a lawyer's office, and an undertakers, until at last when the funeral was over an exhausted Carmen Martinez returned to her apartment with her children and Mrs. Rios.

During the church membership classes, for which she soon enrolled, Carmen made more friends than at any other time in her life ; and when the Church Life Committee had approved her admission and asked the customary question, ' What work do you want to do in the church?' her answer was ' Everything!'

Just one year later, in 1952, she was elected by the congregation to 104th Street's Church Council. This Council's eight lay members, with two permanent Group Ministry members, was responsible for the over-all church programme and for the relation of the church to the other three Parish churches and to secular agencies in East Harlem. Every second Sunday, after morning worship, the Council met in the hall beside the church ; and after ejecting and re-ejecting the small boys and girls who invariably wished to play in what was their Sunday School, the Councilmen would have coffee before the lay chairman opened the meeting with prayer.

Eighteen months after her election to the Church Council,

Carmen was asked to serve on 104th Street's Church Life Committee. This Committee was elected at the annual congregational meeting, and it left the Church Council free to concentrate on administration by taking responsibility for the church membership course, the examination of new members, the forms of worship, and for calling on the sick.

A year later, when Carmen became Chairman of this Committee, it undertook a thorough examination of the meaning of worship, and with the approval of the pastors and congregation, made valuable changes in the service of Holy Communion and in the prayers for the sick. This underlined the increasing importance of the rôle of the laity. No doubt fundamental policy decisions were still left to the Group Ministry; no doubt the voice of the pastors rightly carried more weight than that of others on most committees; but lay men and women now gave a lead in many crucial spheres of church life.

It was not surprising that Carmen was soon elected to one of the Parish Council's committees which supervised such Parish-wide concerns as Christian Action, worship, the farm, and so on. She became a member of the Parish Worship Committee, and was soon deeply involved in the planning of a Parish retreat on 'The Meaning of Christmas'.

'I didn't know what I was letting myself in for when I left Puerto Rico for New York!' she says. Her progression from church member to church Councilman, and then to the Parish Council's Worship Committee, brought out the very best gifts she had; and it meant that she knew what she was talking about when on Laymen's Sunday, 1954, she preached the sermon on the theme, 'We are members of the Body of Christ'; for, like so many very different residents, she had become a responsible member of that Body, and was exercising her own special gifts which were as vital to the church as the gifts of the hand were vital to the body.

Sam Rogers and Carmen Martinez were typical of the three hundred people who had become full members of the Parish by the spring of 1954. Nearly all of them had joined the church for the reason that the youth leader, Bill Cooper, gave: 'My real reason for joining the Parish,' he said, 'was because I found the church was interested not just in preaching but in *people*. In the Parish I found men and women who did more than sit down in church on Sundays and listen. I found they put religion into action. This was what I'd been looking for. And I jumped in with both feet.'

Bill Cooper's attitude is easy to misunderstand. He, and others like him, were not just finding creative outlets for their energies ; although if that were all that could be said, a great deal would have been achieved. Nor were they just finding a focus for their loyalties which helped improve their lives and the life of society ; although again, if that were all, it would have been a great accomplishment. What they were finding, in fact, was that God was forging them into an instrument with which to remake a corner of his world. And this, of course, is another way of saying that they were becoming the Church. They were not just ' coming to church '. There was far more to it than that. They were becoming the Church.

12. HIGH DRAMA

Those who were becoming the Church in East Harlem were responding to a Gospel which they heard in preaching, which they met in action, and which they saw in drama. Perhaps that drama was most gripping during Lent; the forty days which led to Easter Sunday.

On Ash Wednesday, 1954, all four churches were filled in the evening. This was the first day of Lent, and everyone had brought the palms which had hung in their homes since the last Palm Sunday. Before each congregation, the leaves were burned to ashes, and one by one, the people came forward to kneel and receive the sign of the Cross, in ashes, on their foreheads.

'Today,' declared the pastor, 'we burn the palms which we waved as we greeted Jesus last Palm Sunday. Just as the palms of joy are turned by the fire into ashes, so our cries of "Hosanna!" are turned by sin into shouts of "Crucify Him!" Ash Wednesday is a solemn day of confession of our sin, and of sorrow for the wrongs we have committed. The ashes which form a cross on our foreheads are symbols of our weakness and of the power of Christ's Cross to transform death into life.'

On Palm Sunday the central act came in the middle of morning worship when everybody held the long leaves high, and a sea of waving palms filled the church as they cried 'Hosanna!' again and again, giving thanks for Christ's coming to men as King. After the service the palms were taken home and hung in a prominent place in the apartment as a reminder of Christ's kingly rule over each family.

The evening of Maundy Thursday was a time when the fine line that separates symbol from reality thinned almost to breaking point. This was the night of Christ's betrayal; the time of the Last Supper.

After preparation for Communion in the church, the people

of one congregation filed out by candlelight into the adjacent
hall. As they entered the room, the pastor washed their hands
in silence. All took their seats at the brown wooden tables on
which the candles glowed. Then came a simple meal of bread
and fish, a family meal in which men and women and children of four or five nationalities were united.

And then the Holy Communion. 'Let us pray,' said the
pastor, and although the rest of the company were silent, there
was the sense that they were praying with him. And after the
prayer, the pastor took a loaf and broke it in two and passed
it to those on either side of him: they each took a fragment,
and the broken bread was passed on round the table in a silence uncommon even in a service of Communion. Then the
cup. The dim light of the candles was reflected in the chalice
as it passed from hand to hand. When it was returned to the
minister, all had partaken of the Supper, and somehow the
silence seemed to have deepened.

Quietly, the pastor read the account of the events on the
night before Christ died. The departure of Judas, 'and it was
night'; after which a candle was extinguished. The betrayal
in the garden, 'all the disciples forsook him and fled'; another candle was snuffed out. Then Peter's threefold denial,
'and he went out and wept bitterly'; only two candles remained. The scourging and the trial before Pilate, 'his blood
be on us and on our children!'; now the low-roofed hall was
lighted by a single flame. 'And they spat upon him and smote
him on the head . . . and led him away to crucify him'—the
last candle died. No one moved in the pitch-black hall; it
almost seemed as though no one even breathed. In the darkness each person was alone with the knowledge that he was
where the first disciples had been: at the table of the Lord,
and also at the betrayal. 'Let us confess our sins before
God; the sins by which we have betrayed our Lord. . . .'
Then silence and darkness again . . . for two long, prayerful
minutes . . . until the service came to a close with the lighting
of the solitary Christ-candle as a flickering sign of Easter
hope. By that one light all left the hall: they passed out
through the chapel where the Bible, the candles, and the altar
cloth were nowhere to be seen, and the tall brown cross was
draped in black with a crown of thorns above it. And so

out into the world beyond, and down the dark streets home.
'And it was night. . . .'

On Good Friday the three-hour watch was kept in the
churches: a time of meditation on Christ's suffering. That
evening, on a vacant lot, a Passion play was enacted before a
crowd of many hundreds. Most of the actors were church
members, and if no one else met Christ in the play, at least
they did—or so some of them said. Maybe they had not been
very regular at worship, but that day several of them had been
in church and knelt there alone. The Negro who was to take
Christ's part had been there a few times; he was serious and
said nothing. The two girls who were to stand beside the cross
had also been there together for a while. And in the evening
the actors were unusually subdued as a big crowd gathered in
the open space where a rough stage had been built against a
wall. There was a good deal of laughing and catcalling during
the opening scenes, but as the story moved into the Garden
of Gethsemane and on to the road to Calvary, the whole
crowd was hushed, and even the few who had taken too much
liquor held their peace. And the moment when the cry went
up, ' Father, forgive them, for they know not what they do!'
a shock went through the motionless crowd, and the silence
that followed could be felt.

Long before dawn on Easter Sunday a motley collection of
vehicles gathered outside each of the churches. There were the
four Parish station-wagons, about ten borrowed private cars,
a lorry or two, and the old school bus. The members assembled, many in their Easter clothes, some in sweaters and
pyjamas under heavy overcoats. Soon the motorcade was
driving up First Avenue en route to Randall's Island in the
nearby East River. Once over the bridge, the vehicles parked
and the people assembled into one long line. At the head of
each congregation a Councilman bore a bright-coloured
banner with the name of the church inscribed in gold.

Along the deserted path they filed as the shadows began to
disperse; they turned left under the Hell Gate railway via-
duct, and there, planted in the grass with the waters of the
East River behind, was a great wooden cross. Behind the

people were the bricks and mortar and tensions of the city:
across the waters a jungle of factories and chimneys. But for
some standing on this patch of green grass, it was as though
they were with Mary on the first Easter Sunday when the
stone had been rolled away.

The two hundred people formed a wide circle round the
cross, beneath which stood the ministers and three Councilmen. There was a prayer of adoration. And then all waited
in silence.

The minutes ticked by . . . Then, slowly, the sun rose over
the low sea cloud and the shadow of the cross reached out
across the grass.

'Jesus Christ is risen from the dead!' came the loud cry
from the pastor.

'He is risen indeed!' the response echoed back from the
city and out across the water.

'Let us praise God with Alleluias!'

'Alleluia! Alleluia! Alleluia!'

And the service of Easter praise moved on until it reached
its triumphant climax:

'The grace of the Lord Jesus Christ is with us.'

And in the silence, from here and there in the crowd, one
heard, 'Amen,' and again and again, the murmur of 'Amen
. . . Amen . . . Amen. . . .'

PART FOUR

DISCOVERY

13. ACCEPTANCE

It was 1954. Six years had passed since the first storefront church had been opened in East Harlem. Those years had been packed with discoveries which had shocked and inspired the Group; discoveries about East Harlem's hidden riches, about life and compassion and God; discoveries which had sometimes overthrown assumptions which they had always held, and which left them asking such questions as 'Does morality matter to God?' The answers had come not so much through argument as through the harsh impact of events.

'Reach!' said the leader of the Parish youth group, levelling a .45 automatic at the storekeeper's stomach. As the man raised his hands, the group's secretary emptied the till, and then the two backed out of the doorway and raced off down the street.

East Harlem's ideas on morality were very different from those of the Parish ministers. Aside from a tiny minority whose strong moral code gave structure to their lives, most people were so poorly educated, so lacking in stable home background, and so influenced by the local climate of injustice and of rackets that they had no clear moral standards at all.

'God don't mind if you sin now and then, Reverend. He just don't want you to make a habit of it.' The 40-year-old Puerto Rican woman was speaking to one of the pastors in her apartment on 104th Street. They had been discussing the question of stealing, but now the subject moved to the son of whom she was so proud. It seemed that although she was not married, she had very much wanted to have a child of her own. She prayed that God would give her a baby, made friends with a married man, and eventually had a son by him. The minister thought that the matter was worrying her.

'If you've sincerely repented . . .' he began. '*Repented?*' she cried. 'I ain't repented! I *asked* the Lord for him! He's a gift from God!'

In such a situation, where do you begin? Maybe in suburbia you can begin with judgment: where men believe themselves respectable and righteous and religious, perhaps you begin where Christ began with the Scribes and Pharisees. But in East Harlem, with its broken reeds which could so easily be crushed, in such a fragile situation, where do you start? The Group believed they were discovering an answer ; it had to be given again and again to innumerable puzzled questioners.

'What do you do?' asked a student volunteer as the Parish workers sat around the farmhouse fire during one of their monthly retreats. 'What do you do when you drop in on the church youth canteen and find a man lying dead drunk on the floor, and a bottle of whisky being passed from hand to hand? Does the church condone this?'

'No, the church does not condone it,' came the slow but decided reply. 'That's why we have a rule that no drunks will be allowed into church dances.' The pastor hesitated, and then went on. 'But we are not primarily instruments of God's judgment , . . and neither was Christ. We can judge in preaching or in counselling—providing we've first felt a greater judgment on ourselves as responsible for the social situation which produces these results. But our ministry is first one of acceptance. Our primary job is to communicate God's forgiveness of just such drunks as you saw in the church canteen. Don't men like him stand a better chance of going straight inside the church than out? And isn't it true that after what happened on Good Friday, the Church of God is open to all, no matter how they may live?'

No matter how they may live . . . One man who used to belong to the Parish was undoubtedly a convert, was not married to the mother of his children, would get drunk with depressing regularity, and rented a room in his apartment to a prostitute. 'What do you do?' the question persisted. And the answer of the Group was becoming quite clear: 'Christ didn't come with a lawbook in his hand to bless only those who would obey it,' said one pastor. 'He came to save those who couldn't save themselves. And this means that East Harlem's moral wrecks are simply the people who stand in the greatest need of the church's love. It means that we accept them exactly where they are and as they are.'

The discovery that their ministry had to involve unconditional acceptance of all men ' exactly where they are and as they are ' had been made by the Group as they faced three things. First, there was the background from which East Harlem's moral chaos sprang. Second, there was the conventional churches' futile response in terms of condemnation. And third, there was the fact that this response was a flat contradiction of the Gospel.

The background to East Harlem's moral turmoil had made it perfectly plain to the Group that they themselves were in no position whatever to condemn. They thought of a boy whose father was a drunkard and whose mother was mentally unstable ; he had been expelled from school for bad behaviour and was trying to forget his problems by taking heroin. There was the seventeen-year-old girl whose mother had left home ' for a few days ' with a man friend, who had since been caring single-handed for three small children, and had now gone out of her mind. There was Charlie, a young man whose father was a thief and whose mother was a prostitute ; he won recognition at home by what he could steal from the stores. And most of East Harlem's adult thieves and addicts and near-demented individuals were what they were for reasons like these, reasons altogether beyond their control. To judge such people was like abusing a baby for being born a cripple.

Yet judgment seemed to be the traditional church's first word in East Harlem. It almost seemed as if the first concern was not to bring the lost sheep home but to keep the lost sheep out in case they impaired the church's reputation for respectability. ' But this attitude that the church is only for respectable people would exclude most of its finest saints,' wrote Don Benedict. ' No one in his senses would call St. Francis a respectable man, for what respectable man would rummage in a garbage can for his breakfast, and what respectable man would embrace a filthy, blasphemous leper? Clearly, Francis was not respectable. And equally clearly, he was redeemed. And when the church realises that it has a greater desire for a respectable community than for a redeemed one, it must also realise that its whole attitude to morality, and its whole conception of the Gospel of Christ, is being called into question.'

The self-deception behind this 'holier-than-thou' attitude lay in the fact that those in the church who condemned the drunk and the harlot were by no means innocent themselves. A girl who was a Sunday School teacher in a nearby church became pregnant, and Bill Webber overheard the matter being discussed by some of her fellow members. 'It's shameful!' declared a Puerto Rican lady. 'And her a leader in the church!' The speaker had five children by the man with whom she had been living for six years ; she had yet to take the step of getting married. This was one of a thousand instances which had forced the Group to the conclusion that East Harlem's prodigals were avoiding their Father's house not because of their Father at all but because of their elder brothers, who were Christian, immoral, without pity and without mercy. It was perfectly clear that of those who applied the rigorous 'Christian' standard, many kept it merely because it was expedient to do so (that was the way to keep your job and to gain social prestige), and even then they kept it only in those areas of life which were open to inspection by others. In other words, they themselves were guilty men. 'And,' asked Benedict, 'if God were as harsh in his judgment of them as they are in their judgment of others, would they themselves be saved?'

Nevertheless, they *were* harsh in their judgment, as many a man like Charlie the thief had discovered for himself. Charlie had been to church once in his life. He had gone, as he said, ' to hear about Christ ', but instead he heard about judgment. He had gone seeking Christ, but, finding the Law, he departed for good without Christ. Such men were being hardened by the church in their lives of crime and wretchedness ; the judgment of the church had separated them from the one community that ought to be able to help them.

An elder in a local Pentecostal church was a woman with a twenty-year-old son called Tiny. She knew that he was using heroin, and she had followed the example of her pastor by bitterly condemning him and warning him of judgment to come. One day she found Tiny's injection kit hidden above the toilet.

' You been usin' that stuff again!' she cried.

' You ain't see me use nothin',' said Tiny sullenly.

' I may not see you use nothin',' she shouted, ' but I can tell when you done it. D'you hear? I can tell!'

And Tiny lost control. ' You see how you is?' he yelled. ' You talkin', and ravin' like that at me. . . . You *make* me use it!'

Such tragic incidents as this convinced the Group that judgment was useless. The moralistic approach would separate them from those they wanted to befriend; it also presupposed the acceptance of a moral code to which, in fact, many East Harlem residents were totally indifferent. As they wrote some time later: ' If we say, " Don't commit adultery," the answer may well be, " Why not?" And if we go on to say, " It's against the Ten Commandments," the reply is, " *The Ten Commandments* was a punk movie, anyway." '

So the approach by way of morality was rejected, partly because it was useless, partly because it was irrelevant, but above all because the pastors slowly realised that morality (with which their own faith had always been involved) often stood in stubborn opposition to the Gospel. After all, they argued, the object of morality is to preserve the status quo, and the object of the Gospel is often to overturn the status quo (' these that have turned the world upside down '). Morality exalted the Law over the Gospel; it forgot that David did not lose the Spirit of God even though he had committed both adultery and murder; it said to the East Harlem girl who had never known her father, who had seen her mother living with several men, and who had no resources or reasons for resisting the offer of affection which left her carrying a baby—to such a love-starved creature, morality declared, ' You can't join the church until you marry the father of your child.' To the girl, morality seemed a cruel mockery. To the Group it seemed a cheap betrayal of the agony of Christ, for he had died ' not to condemn the world, but that the world, through him, might be saved.' On the one hand, the church seemed to say to the world, ' Christ alone can put your life straight '; and on the other hand, it said to the addicted convert, ' But before you can belong to the church, you'll have to put your own life straight.' It proclaimed from the pulpit, ' The Cross is the power of God unto salvation,' and then it directed men to find their power not in the Cross but in themselves.

The pastors saw that this was a plain denial of the Gospel, a denial of the fact that God's attitude to men simply does not depend upon men's attitude to God. They thought of Paul on the Damascus road when Christ stopped him in his tracks, forgave him outright, and made him an apostle before he even had a chance to repent. They remembered Christ hanging on the Cross, praying for his unrepentant crucifiers: ' Father, forgive them, for they know not what they do.' These were events far removed from the world of morality, a world whose irrelevance lay in the fact that it had no power at all. By contrast, the Group declared, the Gospel is a Gospel of power. It is not a demand but a gift ; it is not the Ten Commandments, nor the Sermon on the Mount, but that only through the power of the living Christ do the Sermon and Commandments become possibilities. God's Good News, they insisted, is not that he calls men to morality but that he calls them to Christ, to the Christ who accepts mean little misers like Zacchaeus, and by that acceptance brings his strength into their lives.

This meant that there was an answer to the question of the woman who opened the door to the visiting pastor on 100th Street : she knew he was aware of the fact that she was living with someone else's husband ; she imagined he had come to condemn her ; and she frowned as she asked, ' Why do you visit *me*?' The pastor was silent for a while before he said, ' If the church were only interested in saints, I guess it would have no place for me.' He paused again, reflectively ; and then : ' It seems to me that God is more interested in loving us than in condemning us.' The woman hesitated, and then managed a faint smile as she said, ' Won't you come in?'

Such a woman, like every other person in East Harlem, was already loved and accepted by Christ ; she might not know it, but she already belonged to him. This was the bed-rock Gospel fact on which the pastors' attitude was based. Christ, they read, ' is above all and through all and in all ': to reject the pimp and the prostitute was to reject the risen Christ ; to accept them was to accept him who said, ' As you did it to one of the least of these my brethren, you did it to

me.' 'We classify men good and bad,' protested Benedict in
a sermon. 'We range them before our judgment seat and
say, " You are a saint. And you are a just man. But you are
a sinner. All this group are sinners. You. And you.
And . . ." But there we stop. For this man standing down
among the sinners has nailprints in his hands . . . He looks
at us. We feel uneasy on our throne. We are afraid. He's
judging us. . . .'

'So the Body of Christ, the church,' wrote the Group,
' must accept those who drink, use narcotics, steal, have out-
of-wedlock sex experience. The church is set in the midst of
the world not to protect its life but to give its life away, that
men may know the Good News of a God who loves them.'

All this exposed the church to the acid judgment of its critics:
' Look at the people they let in! What kind of church is
this?' It was a church that was soon to discover much more
about Christian ethics. But at least it was a church that was
earning the same abuse that Jesus bore when he accepted
racketeers and prostitutes. And at least it was a church that
was bearing fruit, as even little children testified.

The Sunday School class had been asked to describe the
kind of people who come to church. ' Big people come to
church,' said one. ' Children come to church,' said another.
' Yes,' a small boy's voice piped up, surely delighting his
Maker's heart, ' and bad people come to church.'

14. MANNA

When he was stopped outside a candy store one day in 1954, Norm Eddy—pastor of 100th Street—thought of an even more heart-warming discovery than that of the Christian approach to ' bad ' people.

' Well, Reverend,' the big Negro said with a friendly smile, ' you been here a few years now. Time you moved on.'

' I'm not moving on,' said Eddy, ' I'm staying.'

' Won't your church let you move on?'

' I don't want to move on. I wanted to come and I want to stay.'

Eddy was thinking partly of his deep sense of vocation; but he was also thinking of the unsuspected riches he was finding in the lives of those around him. As with the other members of the Group, his early impressions of the district as a wilderness grew stronger the longer he worked there. But at the same time he was discovering treasures and achievements he had never dreamed were there. They astonished him, humbled him, and inspired him beyond words.

The achievement of La Guardia in emerging from East Harlem to become the Mayor of New York City was common knowledge to all. But his was thought to be an isolated triumph. It was news to hear that there were men who had fought their way from a crowded local tenement through high school and college to graduate as doctors and lawyers.

Each one of these was an exception; together they formed a very small minority. But this minority existed, and it contained a few who even returned to the district to work. Moreover, the ministers had come to know a larger minority of young men who had once been vagrant members of warring gangs but who were now skilled workers and were settling down as happily married family men. Again, they were a minority; but they were there, and the question was ' How?'

The answer to the question lay partly in the men themselves, but also in the emotional resources of the district. These vital elements which the Group was discovering had

held and sustained such men through years of agonising
tensions. Without them, they could hardly have survived.
What were these treasures? They are hard to define, though
such surprising words as warmth and gaiety and colour and
song may help. Whatever they were, they did nothing at all to
cancel out the atmosphere of hate and fear, for that still
existed—as it exists today—side by side with these great
riches which perhaps can only be described in terms of life
on East Harlem's streets.

On the third really hot day in May 1954, Billy, a mischiev-
ous thirteen-year-old, decides the time has come to start one
of East Harlem's traditional summer sports. In his bright
scarlet T-shirt and old blue jeans he gets a wrench from a
friend on 100th Street and advances on the nearest fire
hydrant.

The atmosphere is heavy, for the concrete has held the heat
through the night, and all those who can have left their stifling
apartments for the almost equally stifling street.

The sight of the boy with the wrench causes a general stir
on every doorstep, and as he approaches the hydrant on the
sidewalk, he is joined by a dozen bright-eyed youngsters who
begin to jump and cheer and clap as he struggles to open the
outlet wide. First a trickle, then a spurt, and then a rush of
water comes forcing itself out over the street at six hundred
gallons a minute. In a moment the difference is felt even in
the houses, for the temperature drops as the water spreads
across the street.

About a hundred boys and girls of every colour and shape
and size come rushing from all directions to paddle and leap
and fight in the flood. A twelve-year-old has knocked both
ends out of a tin can and fits it over the hydrant's outlet,
directing the jet on to the ground. Now he slowly points the
can higher and higher until, amid excited screams, the strong
jet is hitting the opposite tenement, and just as it is about to
pour in through the open windows, shouts and threats of adult
vengeance persuade him to play the jet along the street where
it cascades down from a height of twenty feet on to children
in their underwear who dart in and out of the gushing foun-
tain or sit down, beaming joyfully beneath it.

Suddenly the jet player looks eagerly up the street. This is what he has been waiting for. The children (including a well-dressed boy, dancing in the downpour beneath an umbrella) clear as if by magic off the street. The car approaches, sounding its horn uncertainly. All the children are shouting and screaming, while their laughing parents gather on the doorstep or crowd the tenement windows. The driver of the car is stepping on the accelerator and winding up his window at the same time, but the force of a direct hit on the glass sends a triumphant jet through the closing half-inch gap. Cheer on cheer from the overjoyed enthusiasts follow the car down the flooded street, but before the echo of applause has died, a youngster comes roller-skating into the water and speeds back and forth, raising waves on either side of his path and laughing and shouting to his delighted friends before he slips and falls headlong in the flood and the whole street rocks with laughter.

This was East Harlem in the summer when its residents sometimes displayed an intoxicating gaiety and people were refreshed by the grace that was not locked up in the church but which was very near at hand in little children.

Among those families which gazed down from their windows there were those that, despite persistent personal misfortunes, maintained a marvellously warm and stable life. The members of the Group had been sustained and renewed by being freely accepted into such strong family circles.

One evening in the early fall of 1954, for example, a pastor and his wife made their way to a rooftop party on a tenement overlooking the East River. Normally, the rooftop is a rather sinister place; here the dope pusher often meets his quarry; here the racketeers may gather, especially in the evenings. But there is safety in numbers, and there would be about twenty at the party, including eight or nine men. The night was fine and the air was unusually clear. High up above First Avenue and 100th Street the people were gathered beside the two-foot safety wall, and amid jokes and laughter, the guests were served with potato crisps and soda or beer or cola. Someone had brought up a record player, and, accompanied by clapping hands and tapping feet and cries of 'Go!', a couple did an intricate dance to the music of drums and guitar. When the dance was done, two of the small boys, grinning cheekily, began to mimic their elders, holding hands and hopping around on the roof while their mothers scolded them, pretending to be cross. At this point coffee and hamburgers with hot cheese dripping from them were brought up from the hosts' tiny apartment, and their friends stood beside the wall or sat down on it, looking up at the clear night sky, or watching the lights from the apartments below, or gazing out over the lights of the cars on the East River Drive to the dark strip of river beyond.

There was nothing unusual about the party; it was all quite simple and normal. But of course that was just the point. This family had its home in a dark tenement in the heart of the narcotics district, its children were exposed to the worst temptations that the area had to offer, and yet it maintained with wonderful dignity a normal family life.

Winter brought its own magic. Just before Christmas 1954, snow fell gently for three successive days, covering vacant lots, sidewalks, and windowsills with a marvellous pure white mantle. On one open space there was a high pile of spruce trees waiting to be sold at a nearby store, and the scent of the snow-covered spruce brought the freshness of the countryside right into East Harlem's streets. In the evenings men gathered in groups here and there, and lighted fires with wood salvaged from discarded crates or from buildings which were being pulled down. Evening fires on vacant lots were a common sight in the district, but in the crisp snow each crackling fire seemed like a bright red dancing miracle which helped to turn East Harlem into a glowing fairy-land. And in the mornings the children made their slides the whole length of the sidewalk, and the air was filled with shouts and screams and laughter and flying snowballs. Looking out of her window, on the morning of Christmas Eve, one of the pastors' wives tried to capture the scene in verse:

> Last night the snow fell
> and children looked this morning
> on a new white world.

Men and women bend their heads
against the whirling, stinging flakes
and stamp through deep piles
with numb feet.

But around them dance children
thoroughly alive
in tattered mittens, men's work gloves
or bare hands blueing in the cold
all all oblivious
pummelling each other,
hurling soft white balls,
rolling snowmen
and dancing,
whirling in the sparkling air
and falling softly into the drifts
laughing and calling,
not the jumbled shouts
of ordinary days
but the note on note
round tones
of children in the snow.

And what mattered was not that, as with so many traces of
beauty in East Harlem, the snow would soon be trampled into
a treacherous, ugly eyesore ; the point was that now, at this
moment, the snow was *there,* and the children's joy was real,
and the adult faces at the windows were not sad but gay and
kindly and alive . . .

So winter reluctantly gives way to spring with its own special
spirit of promise.
   On the first warm evening it is as though the whole block
stands on the edge of a new beginning. The tensions and
hatreds and fears of group for group seem to be forgotten ; at
rare times such as this they are mercifully submerged. Everyone comes out on the doorstep: the women in bright prints
or black dresses, the men in slacks and shirt sleeves and, often,
in their slippers. A few sit on kitchen chairs, but most sit on
the tenement steps, talking quietly. Children stand around the
edge of the group or else sit on the steps beside their parents,

who slip their arms around them and kiss their hair or hug them affectionately before they run off once again to play ball with their friends. Work has been put aside for the day. Everyone is relaxed.

'*Ten cuidado!*' a mother calls out to her ten-year-old boy. But Pancho ignores her call to take care, and continues to climb the fire escape of the empty building next to the church. '*Ten cuidado!*' she calls again before shrugging her shoulders helplessly, and everyone smiles because the boy is old enough to take care of himself.

From the corner of Second Avenue comes the 'Ting-ting!' of an ice-cream truck's bell, and a boy in a red-and-white check shirt abandons a group playing marbles on the sidewalk and runs to join the children crowding round to buy ice cream.

On the steps leading up to his apartment, Don Benedict sits with two middle-aged addicts, talking, laughing now and then, watching the colourful scene. From down the street there is the sound of a group of Negroes singing together endlessly. The little knots of people on the doorsteps have an air of contentment; discussion goes easily from one to the other. This evening they seem to have time . . .

'Kinda different from your home town, Reverend Don?' asks Alfonso, surveying the street.

'Guess so. In my home town people don't have time. They're always on the move, trying to catch up with themselves.'

They look across the street at a group of boys who have been standing there for an hour, beating out rhythms on the mudguards of a black Ford car.

'See those kids?' asks Alfonso. 'They're doin' nothin'. And they're not bothered by it.'

'That's how it is in Puerto Rico,' declares Julio, rubbing two days' growth of beard with the back of a horny hand. 'On the island there's no movies, no pool. There's not even work, man. Least not till the last few years. The kids, they grow up jus' standin' aroun'. Nothin' to do except the bar and hang aroun'.'

'Like I say,' says Alfonso. 'They're not bothered. That's how life is in Puerto Rico. Take the summer I leave the island. A guy from New York, he stops his car in my village.

Tourist, I guess. He's on vacation with his camera, and he takes a shot of the avocado tree outside our house. Now that guy says, " You chose a good place to plant that avocado tree, friend." And I say, " No, no one planted that avocado tree. Maybe ten years ago my Anna, she threw out some garbage with some seeds in it. That's why there's an avocado tree there," I say.'

The three men chuckle with the air of those enjoying a private joke.

Across the street a stout Negro mother comes heavily out of her tenement door and sinks down beside her sister on the steps. ' Ai, yai, yai!' she sighs, and takes a deep breath of the evening air. She has been trapped indoors all winter by the cold, but now the spring has brought her freedom. She expands visibly.

So the evening slips by. It begins to get dark. The concrete looks more friendly in the lamplight ; more mysterious. There are shadows . . . By eleven all the children are in bed except for the babies asleep in their mothers' arms. Now the parents relax (if they know where their teenage children are), and they sit and talk until well after midnight, recalling their days in a Puerto Rican village or their childhood in a small town in South Carolina. In the lamplight they talk more freely. They are more at ease with one another. Those who don't live here have long since gone home. These are the people who go upstairs to sleep. These are the people who understand.

' 'Night, folks,' says Benedict to his friends on the steps, making his way up to his apartment.

' 'Night, Reverend,' come the quiet replies.

And the pastor goes in to lie awake on his bed for a while, grateful for manna in the wilderness.

15. LEARNING FROM THE WORLD

Of course manna is no luxury. The bread which the children of Israel found on their wilderness pilgrimage was a life necessity. So it was with East Harlem's scanty 'manna'; it was hard to discover amid so much despair and hate, but when it was found, it proved itself a real necessity as it reshaped the Parish workers' attitude to life, and to human love, and even to God himself.

Sometimes East Harlem struck at the roots of some members' hard-won philosophy. 'My whole life has been conditioned by the fact that winter is coming,' said one of the staff, ' and I have to prepare the woodpile to survive. But the Puerto Rican doesn't have to prepare for anything. Poverty is often grinding and tragic, but it is accepted as normal; and some succeed in living marvellously useful lives.' Not that grinding poverty was seen as a goal to strive after. The point was that the affluent life, with its stress on annuities and keeping your suit out of pawn, was called into question by East Harlem; and the Sermon on the Mount made sense in terms of the lives of at least some local residents: 'For a man's life consisteth not in the abundance of things which he possesseth. . . .'

' Maybe,' wrote the Parish nurse as she thought of the fine family lives of some local people, and also of the Group's concern for improving material conditions, 'maybe we are exposing East Harlem people to something less than some of them already have. If our emphasis is on the physical environment (which is the first thing to hit us) and its improvement (which is the obvious thing to do about it), we are repeating a basic plank of middle-class morals: i.e., that *things* are very important. In one breath we may say to the middle classes, " The cult of things is an abomination "; in the next breath we may assert that material improvement is the primary need of the poor.'

But there were those in East Harlem who taught the Group by their example that while their material need might be acute, they had needs which went far deeper: the need for human friendship and love, the need for community. They demonstrated this basic need by their reluctance to leave their few friends in a rotting tenement for what was often the impersonal, prison-like atmosphere of new housing projects; by their desire, in other words, to choose people rather than things; and in this way, as one pastor testifies, ' they gave a lesson for life to those of us whose middle-class philosophy had blinded us to a crucial Gospel truth.'

Yet other lessons penetrated deeper. There was the lesson of love, for example.

'When I first came to East Harlem,' says one minister, ' and children came and ran to me and kissed me, I thought, " These children are starved of love." It took a long time to realise that it was *I* who was starved of love, and it was these kids who poured it out on me from the natural warmth of their lives.' It was true that life on the block soon drove their love deep down beneath hard layers of frustration and resentment and suspicion. But at least for a few gay, wonderful years their love was let loose on East Harlem's streets so that all those with eyes to see might realise that this was what was meant by ' becoming as little children'.

Yet amazingly enough, this quality was not drained out of every adult. There were some among the thousands of confused, defeated residents whose love was like a ray of hope that flickered in the dark. There was ' Doc ', for one. In his chemist's shop on 100th Street, this gruff, dour figure presided. Doc Idell was a plump, bald sixty-year-old who sometimes cracked wry jokes with his customers, but more often yelled abuse at them and pretended that he meant every word. Doc kept four chairs in his shop: they were reserved for any elderly men who cared to come and sit and maybe talk for an hour or more. There was no place in East Harlem for elderly men; they felt unwanted, and Doc knew this; and he did something about it. He also employed a few young boys to run errands and deliver medicines; he took them on not so much because he needed them but in order to give them a chance to feel that they mattered, a chance to hold down a job. He learned Spanish in order to talk with the youngsters and elderly Puerto Ricans who brought their problems to him. 'And,' says Norm Eddy, 'if a boy needed two letters to get into the Navy, he went first to Doc, and second to the Parish. He was loved by everyone on the block. He was a Jew. And he was a judgment on the church, and an inspiration to it.'

There were those in the Group who asserted that such love was not enough; that while it could certainly ease many burdens, it could not accomplish the Gospel miracle of bringing the life of God into the lives of men. But there were others who held that it was equally true that without the kind of practical love which they had seen in Doc, the Gospel would never begin to reach men's hearts; in fact, it would not even be the Gospel.

No doubt it was true that for every Doc Idell there were a thousand Edward Emmanuel Washingtons whose experience had taught them to trust no one and to care only for themselves. And yet, like the rare blades of grass that pushed their way through the concrete of the teeming streets, there was a handful of people on every crowded block whose love never seemed to run dry.

'Hi, Cheewawa! Come up!' a woman would call from her third-floor window to a bleary-eyed little man who was sweeping the sidewalk with a cast-off broom. Cheewawa (which means a tiny, hairless Mexican dog) would look up and then climb the stairs to receive a plate of soup, and perhaps an old pair of slacks. He would spend his time sweeping the streets and cleaning the cars in the hope of being paid a few cents; and as the weekend approached, he would become more active, for this was when people would want someone to get drunk with them, and 'Maybe I'll be the lucky guy,' he would say. And when he returned from one of his periodic weeks in jail, he would always get a welcome 'Hi, Cheewawa!' from the children who would crowd eagerly around him. 'This makes me feel so good when I come back,' he told a pastor on one such occasion, before he shambled off with a passer-by who had been out of work for several months, whose principal worries were money and food and who had offered him a meal and a bed for the night in his dingy home. And as the pastor turned away, thinking of his own attempts to meet that kind of need, he found himself recalling Jesus' contrast of the well-to-do with the poor, great-hearted widow: 'They all contributed out of their abundance; but she out of her poverty has given all she had.'

The point was that while Doc Idell and Cheewawa's benefactor had no church connection at all, their lives were still touched by him whom St. John describes as 'the Light that lightens *every* man that comes into the world.' And when the Light of the world approached his church through East Harlem's people, he exposed not only the weakness of their pilosophy and love; he also penetrated deep down beneath their clerical preserves and undermined their faulty doctrine too.

It was so in regard to the Group's approach to immorality, an approach which had tended to follow the conviction that 'our first job is to communicate God's acceptance' rather than his judgment. That conviction was not destroyed: if anything, it was strengthened. But a strong dimension was added to it by such local people as Luis Cortez, the young Puerto Rican who was now working full time with 102nd Street church.

When his group of teenagers burst into the church hall one evening, Luis took one look at the crate of stolen apples which they carried so triumphantly and his response did not look like 'acceptance'. 'So!' he blazed out furiously. 'You meet here in the church and you go out and raid the stores. You think you're smart. I tell you, you're fools! One day you'll do this and the cops'll come. And when they come they'll shoot. They won't care whether they plug you in the leg or in the heart.' The group stood motionless as Luis glared round at them. 'And listen. I'll tell you something. You can't believe in God and then go and steal someone's apples. It's *wrong*. You just can't do it!' His voice was rising with anger. 'You know what you are? You're all *thieves*! That's what you are. Every one of you's a thief!' and he pointed at them one by one, his accusing finger jabbing the air just short of every startled face. 'You're a *thief*! *Thief*! *Thief*! *Thief*! *Thief*! . . .'

This was authority and ministry and grace, and, undoubtedly, judgment. But it was a judgment which did not reject the boys who continued to meet with Luis in the church. In other words, Luis still accepted those who were thieves although his judgment of them was absolute. The question was whether this was a lesson which could be applied by ministers who unlike Luis came from a more privileged background: had they the right to judge? The answer came in terms of concrete events.

On a rainy Saturday evening one of the pastors turned into 104th Street and stopped short in surprise at the sight of a member of his church; the man was very drunk.

'Hi, Flacco,' said the minister to the gaunt, wild-eyed figure who stood blocking his path.

Flacco gazed back sullenly, and then, for some strange, twisted reason, burst out with the sudden protest.

'Listen, you dirty priest. This Jesus guy. He's a swine!' He swayed nearer the pastor and then cried out again, 'Jesus is a swine! Jesus is a swine!' Flacco was shouting at the top of his voice and his words were like slashes from a razor's edge, leaving the pastor wounded and weak and utterly confused. How to defend his Lord against this man? How to defend God's Son? Then suddenly he felt convinced that his job was not to defend. His rôle was to accept; to accept old Flacco precisely as he was, without hint of condemnation. 'Jesus is a swine!' The pastor's whole attitude changed. He relaxed. He stood there in a drizzle of rain, feeling as though the cries were biting deeply into his flesh, but believing, as Flacco finally shambled off, that God's will had been done.

But had it? It turned out that at all events Flacco's will had not been done. The pastor called on him next day.

'Come in, Reverend,' he said gravely, motioning him to sit down on an unmade bed beside the stove. They both sat in silence for what seemed like five minutes, before Flacco looked up and asked, 'Why didn't you knock me down last night?' He really meant what he said. He meant it, perhaps, because he wanted boundaries to be set round his undisciplined life, and he wanted the security of knowing they were boundaries which must not be crossed. Flacco had publicly confessed his faith in Christ, and if he abused his Lord, he hoped that his pastor would knock him down.

'And is that not what Jesus did?' a pastor's wife wrote after this event. 'He did not knock men down—or perhaps he did, when he threw them out of the temple—but he certainly did more than accept them absolutely. In fact, his absolute acceptance was matched by an absolute demand. He said to the woman taken in adultery, " I do not condemn thee." But he also said, " Go, and sin no more." He said in effect to Peter after he had denied him, " I accept you with all your denials." But he also said, " Will you accept *me* with all my demands?" ' In other words, Christ accepted Peter as a man and he asked Peter to accept him as God. Not that Christ's acceptance depended on Peter's embracing his demands. The first was a fact ; only the second was a question. But the demand was there ; and it made Peter an apostle and a martyr and a man.

This way of both acceptance and judgment called for great sensitivity ; sometimes it called for great courage.

When Flossie Borgmann rebuked the youths who invaded the Parish office and stole her equipment, they responded by throwing rotten tomatoes through her apartment window on to her papers and furniture and curtains and clothes ; when she persisted in leavening her friendship with judgment, they dropped lighted matches down the mailbox where she had mailed the Parish letters ; and when she took one of them by the collar and thrust him outside the office door, he turned and struck two vicious blows full in her face, and sent her reeling backwards over a box to land flat out on the floor. This did not shake her determination to discipline the youths ; but because she believed that her judgment had to be the other side of a stronger acceptance, it seemed to her the most natural thing to invite the ringleaders to her apartment on the evening after she had been beaten up. There they had a good chicken dinner, and, as she says, ' We talked about what the church was and why it was necessary to keep them out of the office. And,' she adds, ' we enjoyed each other and we became fast friends.'

People like Luis and Flacco and Flossie Borgmann's friends taught the Group that judgment alone could drive men away from God and from the church ; so could acceptance if it treated them as children and failed to respect them. What was needed was an acceptance which loved them and held on to them, and also a judgment whose demands treated them as men. Together, acceptance and judgment could turn unruly vagrants into responsible men who knew that if they ceased to be responsible, they would still be accepted by God and by his church; but who also knew—however dimly—that their very manhood depended on their accepting God's demands.

But there was a more devastating and rewarding lesson which the city had to teach. Archie Hargraves was learning it in Chicago as the Parish there grappled with the hopelessness of alcoholics and drug addicts. But we need look no further than East Harlem to see that the lesson which was being learned was that through their needy neighbours, God was pronouncing his judgment not merely on society at large but on the Group, on their home congregations, on the nation-wide denominations, on the Church of Christ itself.

' Truly to hear the cry from the Cross in our time,' a Parish worker wrote, ' truly to know our guilt in the Crucifixion, the church must listen to the muffled cry of a suffering world. And to the extent that it " hears " East Harlem, the Parish hears the Word of God.' What Word of God were such men hearing?

They were hearing God's Word when a young Puerto Rican casually remarked, ' You can still get a guy killed here any time. You hire a kid who's needing dope and you promise him a fix. For a fix he'll do anything. Then if you want to make sure nobody knows about it afterwards, you give him an overdose and that does it. They call it suicide.'

To those with ' ears to hear ' this was God's terrible Word of judgment on a society whose neglect was to blame for making murder commonplace. But if God's judgment fell on the whole of society, it fell with special force on the church which had failed to leaven society with the love and the law of Christ, with the result that ' You can still get a guy killed any time.'

Moreover, this Word was heard not only in speech but also in action.

One March evening a youth stepped out of the shadows near an East Harlem community centre. He raised a stripped-down .22 gun and fired five times at a group of teenagers. Three of them fell to the ground. Two were badly wounded. One was dead.

Was this also the Word of God? The Group came to believe that it was, because while the answer to violence was partly one of social reform, the final answer was a change of heart on the part of individuals and groups. That is to say, it was the answer of the Gospel. But the Gospel had been all but withheld from East Harlem. The church had virtually abandoned the district and had carried its Gospel mainly to the middle classes, leaving those whom Jesus called ' the least of these my brethren ' to the mercies of racketeers. So for those who were willing to hear, God's Word of judgment came to a church that had betrayed Christ's brethren ; it came in the cynical, perfectly truthful assertions of men on the street, and it came in the high-pitched crack of a stripped-down .22 gun.

And as ears became attuned, the note of judgment was heard again and again, as when a janitor asked, ' What are you guys doing here? I thought the church only went where there was money?' And God's rebuke came to one minister as he told the Good Samaritan story to a serious youngster on 100th Street. ' Why do you suppose the priest walked by on the other side?' he asked. The teenager looked up thoughtfully and said, ' I guess he knew the guy had already been robbed.' Why, the Parish workers asked themselves, was his picture of the priest no different from his picture of the racketeer? And the obvious answer was that the only world he knew was one in which men exploited the defenceless and the weak. The church had altogether failed to show him a different kind of world. And so his devastating answer had the force of Jeremiah's protest: ' Thus saith the Lord against the pastors, " Ye have abandoned my flock, and have not visited them, and have strengthened the hands of evildoers." '

So it was no wonder that a Parish pastor could remark soberly, ' When I stand up beside an East Harlem boy before a judge I know that I'm under judgment too. And so is the whole church.'

' Painfully then,' a Parish report concluded, ' the deepest sense of guilt for the sin of East Harlem must rest with the East Harlem Protestant Parish, with the Christian Church.'

Perhaps it was this healthy, realistic sense of their own guilt that made the Parish staff so willing to learn from East Harlem. In doing so they discovered that the impact of the world can be the impact of God himself: that just as the Bible could say of the pagan monarch, Cyrus, ' He is God's

Shepherd and shall do all his pleasure,' so the Parish workers could declare from their experience, 'East Harlem is God's Shepherd and shall do all his pleasure.'

George Todd cut through to the heart of the matter when he wrote from his Parish church on 106th Street: ' Engagement in politics, legislative testimony, and struggles for better housing lead us into areas where God is already at work: these are places where we can meet him: here we find him doing what we testify he does when we say the Creed on Sunday. Hence we go not first of all with crusading zeal but with humble looking and listening for the living word offered to the church.'

In other words, like all the ancient prophets, one takes a concrete situation, hears in it the voice of God, and then turns to the people and declares, ' Thus saith the Lord. . . .'

' Within its own life,' George Todd went on, ' the church hears the Word of God as offered in the Scriptures, in preaching, and in sacraments. But it is to the world of which the church is part that we look for God's actions—creating, governing, redeeming—and in them we hear a living word, saving us and the world now. It is then,' he concluded, ' that the man outside the church, the man in need, the imprisoned, the homeless man, becomes a bearer of Christ for us. Christ comes to meet us, blessing us at the places where crosses stand in the world around us. More grace-laden than any gift we might bring from our privileged place within the church may be the gift God offers us of himself, met in those who confront us with their need.'

16. THE GROUP

There can be no doubt at all that if the Group was learning a great deal from East Harlem, East Harlem was learning much more from the Group. That was why four strong congregations were taking root in a wilderness where the church had failed so many times before.

The Group Ministry (known also as 'the staff') is completely sincere when it gives the laity the credit for the growth of such a vital church. But this book is not written by the Group—because, rightly or wrongly, its members insist, ' We lack the perspective.' So the reader must bear with the author's judgment that if the staff lack perspective in no other realm, they certainly lack it in the realm of taking credit ; for the basic explanation for the strong life of the Parish surely lies with the Group Ministry.

This is a dangerous assertion. Let the reader declare, as the writer does, that the staff were the pioneers who brought new life to the wilderness, and these normally patient men and women will all but destroy him with a blistering fire of denial. This is not mock modesty. It is identification : it is the result of being so much at one with your neighbour that matters of credit or blame become an impertinence ; and if well-meaning strangers set the Group on a pedestal, they are separating them from their best friends, and attacking that which is most precious to them. Nevertheless, the writer, like all who have worked with the Parish staff, must side with East Harlem's laity by asserting that, humanly speaking, the Parish would not exist today had it not been for the coming of the Group.

If the church was to be born in a place like East Harlem, someone had to take the initiative. And in practice that meant that the initiative could be taken either by a group or by a lone minister. But the stark historical facts proved conclusively that in such a district, no normal man had the strength to last for more than a few years on his own in an outgoing, all-embracing ministry. The job of training an infant church and at the same time of reaching out to those beyond nearly always ended in retreat—a psychological retreat to a pulpit-centred programme, or, much more often, a physical retreat to suburbia which left the slum church looking once more for a minister. The tragedy was that while a procession of pastors brought a wide variety of emphases, it failed altogether to give that continuity without which no church could mature; it failed to bring that sense of wholeness which the church was meant to bring; in fact, it added confusion to confusion, and all in the name of Christ.

By 1954 it looked as though the only answer was a Group Ministry. This discovery was important to people far beyond East Harlem. It was a discovery that mattered greatly to those national church leaders who had been watching the work for six years; their hope was that it might provide a pattern for the church in other city jungles. Some of them had become convinced that it did; they believed that only such a group had the resources that were needed for the job.

East Harlem's Group Ministry had the time and the talents to help bring a church into being, and also to train it and lead it in serving the district. It could reach out into the community and form its congregations; it could also provide, as it were, a fertile soil into which those congregations could sink their roots and from which they could draw their life until they achieved maturity.

Moreover, the Group Ministry could provide continuity on a long-term basis even though individuals might sometimes have to leave its ranks. This was illustrated vividly in May 1954, when Don Benedict left East Harlem. He went to found a similar Parish in Cleveland. He went at a time when the work in East Harlem was at a critical stage. The contribution which he had made to the Parish was absolutely basic: it mattered enormously. But fundamentally his going did not matter. The ministry went on. Had Benedict's been a lone pastorate, the work would undoubtedly have come to a stop. But despite the loss of his outstanding gifts of leadership, despite the loss of his deeply Christian insight, the life and work of the Parish went on. It lagged momentarily, to be sure. But then it forged ahead.

The fact that East Harlem's ministry was a group ministry gave the kind of assurance and continuity which was basic to the Gospel that it preached. That continuity gave parishioners a sense of security which they did not have before. It gave them a deep sense of confidence when the 'abiding Gospel' which they heard was reflected in the abiding ministry which they saw. They knew that the church, with its concern for the whole of their life, was really established among them. They knew it was there to stay. As a twelve-year-old boy shyly testified, 'It's like having a friend you know ain't never gonna move away.'

East Harlem's Group Ministry was six years old, and it certainly looked as though it was 'never gonna move away'. The members of the staff could persevere because the Group gave them the three gifts they needed most. The first of the three was strength.

The strength of many residents was drained away in a constant effort to escape the tensions of the district. The first task of those who went to minister there was to identify themselves with their neighbours in everything except this attempt to evade the pressures. The reason for their being there was to face the pressures, to grapple with them, and to try to do something creative about them. 'This identification which we seek,' Webber noted, 'is that of a swimmer with a drowning man. We must feel the same swift currents, the same threats to existence, and yet be able to point the way to the shore.' But to be able to point the way to the shore called for extraordinary strength. Few lone ministers possessed such strength. Even the apostles had been sent out in twos and threes, for stresses which could not be borne alone could be borne by a group, by the church. And they could be borne in such a way as to strengthen the life of a group; for the same strains which would drive one man away could unite and inspire and invigorate a team, and confirm its members in their calling.

One night in 1954 one of the pastors was near the end of his resources. His congregation was angrily divided over the election of a church Councilman. His youngest child was in hospital with acute pneumonia. The youth group in his church had become inexplicably hostile. For the last four nights his sleep had been broken by senseless after-midnight calls. He was physically exhausted, emotionally overwrought, and spiritually bankrupt. The theoretical observer might assert that he should simply ' take it to the Lord in prayer ' and rise refreshed. The experienced participant will know that the surest way to the Lord is through his brother. And to his brother the distracted disciple went.

His brother was the gentle John Crist, who welcomed him with his invariable greeting, ' Peace !' As 104th Street's co-pastor, John was a man with a priestly function. In this situation that function was first expressed simply by sitting beside his friend, accepting him in silence, being on-his-side. It involved hearing his confession of despair, of disillusion, of doubt, of disbelief. And then it involved doing that which his brother was constantly called upon to do for others and which normally was never done for him: it involved offering him the message of the Gospel, of forgiveness, of renewal, of Christ ; assuring him of that which undergirded his whole ministry, of the fact that he was accepted and needed and loved by God and by his friends.

Here in this comradeship, strength and reality were found. The man who was bringing the Gospel to East Harlem did not refuse it for himself. He was willing to be served by his brother, for he knew that unlike some parishioners John Crist did not regard him as a superman ; he regarded him as his neighbour, as his fellow member of a group which strength-ened him when all went wrong by bearing his burdens for him, and which strengthened him when all went well by simply being there beside him.

In such ways as this, the members of the staff gained the strength to stay in East Harlem, to identify themselves with the turbulent life of the district and yet to keep their reason whole.

The second gift which the Group gave its members was the rare gift of freedom. ' I'm a prisoner,' complained a lone pastor in a nearby Harlem church. ' I'm chained to a host of jobs which must be done and for which I have had little training. And I'm not free to give time to those jobs which I know I can do well.' This man was the administrator, the negotiator with social workers, the leader of worship, the organiser of protests, the visitor in the home, and the one who had to have a grasp of local legislation, of the problems of school boards, of teenage gangs, and of men on welfare. He was overwhelmed by the need to be universally gifted. And not being universally gifted, he sometimes took refuge in despair, sometimes in dictatorship. Both led to frustration: for him and for his church. Both led away from the freedom which the Gospel ought to bring.

The members of the Group Ministry were no less individualistic than such a man as this. In fact, they themselves declare, 'It is precisely because we are such a group of individualists with conflicting views on many issues that we feel so keenly the need of a Group Ministry to hold our individualism in line and to supplement the abilities of one another.'

It was this supplementing of one another's abilities that was liberating the members from the 'need' of being omnicompetent. It freed each to exercise his own particular gift—as a pastor, youth leader, administrator, worker with addicts. As one member said, 'The glory of the Group for me is this: I need no longer feel perfect. I can see my particular gift being enriched by the gifts of other members, and I can see the gifts of the whole Group bearing lasting fruit. This means that I no longer feel ultimately needed. And that brings freedom to my ministry, freedom to be myself, to be the pastor I am meant to be. And that in turn brings gaiety. It means I can rejoice in East Harlem. I can laugh.'

Strength and freedom. And the third gift the Group gave its members was the crucial gift of direction. 'We believe,' Don Benedict had said six years before, 'that East Harlem's primary need is for leadership.' But as the life of the Parish developed, the urgent question had to be faced: Leadership in which direction?

'We need to keep things on a *Christian* level!' one member of the staff would often protest, for again and again, in the pressure of overwork and of insistent demands upon their time, the ultimate goal of the Parish would be blurred, and the will of East Harlem would take the place of the will of Almighty God.

But the fact that the Parish had not a solo minister but a group ministry meant that these unconscious changes in direction did not often remain unchallenged for long. As we shall see, the Group sometimes wandered down attractive byways that led it far from the Kingdom of God; but its main chance of getting back on the road to that Kingdom lay in the fact that there was usually at least one member who acted as a painful irritant, facing his friends with their failings, and helping them find the right direction again, the direction towards their Lord.

Through such an irritant ministry the Group members were constantly recalled to their need of faith and love and God, and were helped to be people who could give themselves —and Jesus Christ—to men.

In 1948 a group of denominational executives had protested, 'We cannot get competent, well-trained men to go into inner-city ministries.' This was their reluctant verdict after years of frustrating experience. But now they had made a discovery. For in the six years which had followed the formation of the Group (and up to the time of writing), there were always more first-class men wanting to work in the Parish than it was able to employ.

And this new situation had had very practical effects: for whatever may be said to minimise the importance of the Group, the fact remains that before it came to this densely populated section of East Harlem, there had been no regular Protestant church there at all. Since its arrival, four vigorous congregations had come to life.

In other words, the Group had at last made the break-through which isolated ministries almost always failed to achieve. It had made it possible for ministers to go and *stay* in the inner-city. It had made it possible for the church to be born and to grow and to mature there. It had given the vision which was inspiring the same thing to happen else-where: in Chicago, in Cleveland, and even in cities overseas.

PART FIVE

STRANGE PILGRIMAGE

17. FAILURE

If the years ahead were to bring dramatic changes, the past six years had brought remarkable results. And because these results could not have been achieved without the coming of the Group, their work was seen as an outstanding success by great numbers of people, including the members of their Administrative Board: 'The appropriate attitude on our part to this project,' wrote Truman B. Douglass to his distinguished colleagues on the Board, ' is the attitude of pupils.'

But some of the Group held a very different view from that of their Board; for by 1955 they were more conscious of failure than success. They outline three perplexing facts which the writer hesitates to record, but does so on the Group's recommendation. They were baffled by three problems which haunted them with a sense of defeat: ' We were almost independent of the laity. We were sharing little more than token powers with the laity. And underlying this kind of failure was the fact that we were often more concerned with our own ideas than with God's; we forgot that the head of the Kingdom which we sought was not a committee but a King.'

The protest about the Group's declining relationships with their parishioners came first from the laity themselves. ' You ministers are always too busy,' a 30-year-old Puerto Rican objected. 'You never drink coffee with me any more. You have your *own* coffee sessions. You just come here now on business.'

Part of the answer to the protest was that the ministers were now deeply involved in a host of responsibilities which gave them little time for drinking coffee with anyone. But they point out that of equal importance was the fact that the Group had grown from three to eighteen members in the last six years, and any coffee drinking was now done more with like-minded Group members than with the laity. In other words, as one member declares, ' The Group had tended to become the focus of our social lives.' And this meant that if the members of the congregations had gone out of existence, the Group could have continued to operate as a self-contained unit. Its members were no longer forced to enter deeply into the laity's ways of thinking and feeling. ' I was with you,' wrote St. Paul to his Corinthian congregation, ' in weakness and in fear and in much trembling.' It was not always so with the Group. They were nearly always able to deal with their parishioners from a position of strength. Unlike Paul, they were not dependent on the laity. They did not need them.

Not that the Group rejoiced in this. It was baffled by it. And it was baffled by much else besides. For not only did the Group tend to form a psychological barrier between its members and the laity; it often formed a frustrating physical barrier which imprisoned them in a multitude of staff meetings when they might have been out on the streets or in the homes, helping meet their parishioners' needs. ' The Group convenes itself an improvident number of times in the course of even a week,' wrote one member in his resignation letter, ' and I resign to be free to engage in East Harlem's concerns rather than continue to be engaged in Group Ministry concerns.' This protest ignored the pastor's need to thrash out his perplexing problems with others in the Group; but it underlined the fact that too much time was being spent in ministering to the Group itself. ' And yet that would have been fine,' says one member with a rueful smile, ' only it left so little time for ministry to East Harlem!'

This tendency to be independent of the laity was symbolised most sharply in the fact that key decisions were all taken by the staff. It would of course have been unrealistic to share all responsibility with the first lay members, some of whom proved to have no more than a nominal allegiance; after all, the lay men and women who had authority in the early church had been trained and tested by Jesus himself for years. But just as Christ's seventy disciples exercised real power even during his ministry, so now there were more than seventy in the Parish who could use such power responsibly. Yet although the Group had steadily increased the authority which they shared with the laity, it was still true that lay members had no say at all in such matters as finance or the employment of personnel.

This would have been bad enough if the Group had had a monopoly of wisdom. ' But this was by no means the case,' says one of the staff. ' We always hired nice people to work in the Parish, but sometimes they were quite irresponsible.'

There was one young pastor who had just left seminary and who was driving a Parish group to Stony Brook, Long Island, for a weekend conference, and ' When I got behind the wheel,' he says, ' I wasn't a minister any more; I was a kid!' It was so hot that he had removed his clerical collar and with open shirt was driving along the Grand Central Parkway at well over the 40-mile limit. But the spell of the speed was suddenly broken when he saw a motor-cycle patrolman in the driving-mirror; the officer was fast overtaking the station wagon, and his object was very clear. Keeping his foot down on the accelerator and with one hand on the wheel, the pastor reached out hastily behind him, groping for the collar which he hoped would prevent his being booked. In his haste he knocked it off the seat and reached frantically down to the floor as the patrolman drew alongside, calling out ' Pull over!' As the station wagon slowed to a halt, the driver was still fumbling for his badge of office, but the law was already at his window, bringing a gale of laughter from the car's back seats with ' Never mind the collar, Reverend. Just let me see your licence.'

' Everyone enjoyed it,' the pastor concludes, ' but no one felt that the Group had chosen a very responsible man.'

It was such small incidents, together with more serious events, that were causing grave concern among the staff and growing discontent among the laity. At a recent Laymen's Conference (1954) the protest had been made, ' We feel that the congregations should have a voice in the selection and dismissal of pastors, and we feel their suggestion should be followed.' But two years later they still had no voice when the Group asked the pastor of one congregation to seek an appointment elsewhere. Many of his church members were deeply distressed when he left, and were determined that he should return. ' Don't worry,' they said to one of their

Councilmen, 'he'll be back if we have anything to do with it.'
The trouble was that in fact they had nothing to do with it.
And he did not come back.

' As we held the reins in such affairs of personnel,' one pastor
declares, ' so most financial matters were entirely in our
hands.'

Normally, their handling of money matters was almost too
meticulous. The bulk of their funds came not from big
denominations but from churches and groups and individuals
scattered across the country, and they recognised their responsibility to use the money with care. But they are the first to
point out that sometimes they failed miserably, as when they
produced the first and only edition of *The Edge,* a Parish
newspaper which was a total failure and which cost several
hundred dollars.

But the fact that, normally, the staff was scrupulously careful in all financial matters was not so much the point. The
point was that although the money had been given to the
church, it was only a fraction of the church, the Group
Ministry, which had any say in the way it was used. Occasionally, one or other of the staff would give the laity a voice
in a major financial matter ; but sometimes even such exceptions ended in bitter resentment. One of the pastors tells how
in 1955 he asked his Church Council to decide how their
benevolent fund should be spent. The Council debated the
matter for an hour, voted on the issue, and reached its conclusion. But the decision was not the one which the pastor
had expected. And so he vetoed it. The result was a furious
explosion. ' What d'you do with a guy like that?' demanded a
Councilman indignantly. ' He's playing games with us!'
' And of course,' says the pastor today, ' the Councilman was
right.'

It was not that such members of the Group believed that they
alone possessed God's Spirit. They believed that every church
member had his own unique gift to bring, and that was why,
through the years, they had steadily increased the realm of lay
authority. But was that realm too small? Some thought it
was: for it was one thing for lay members to share in the
choice of a Councilman and of how church time should be

spent ; it would be quite another thing for them to share in the choice of a minister and of how church funds should be spent. It seemed to some that as this was not being done, the laity were taken much less seriously than Paul had taken those Christians in Corinth, who after eighteen months were left in charge of a church which took root in a wilderness very like East Harlem. For such pastors as John Crist the contrast meant that ' We are demonstrating our imperialistic view of Christian mission, we are stifling the laity and usurping the rights of the church.'

It was true—and the fact cannot be overemphasised—that without the Group Ministry the church would not have come into existence. But ' existence ' was not the same as ' life ', as the staff told their Administrative Board in 1955: ' The Group Ministry, which is intended to be the umbilical cord that will nourish the birth of a new Christian community, can in fact strangle the infant by choking lay initiative and giving professional teamwork a higher priority than pastor-Parish teamwork.'

And the crucial question which held the key to the problems of the Group was this: ' *Why* was the infant being strangled? Why did the staff not act on a conviction which many of its members held?'

The reason was simple. The conviction that the laity should share all power was held by many members. It was not held by all. And both those who held it and those who rejected it did so not as a matter of opinion but as a matter of belief, of conscience. And because it was a matter of conscience, the overburdened members of the Group found it very hard indeed to discuss it at all, let alone reach a common mind upon it ; for while differences in doctrine could be rungs on the ladder to truth, they could also be rungs on the ladder to despair when they touched off explosive disagreements every time that they were raised. And so the lay members' status went unchanged. The strangling of ' the infant ' went unchecked.

It would, of course, have been astonishing if there had been no serious differences, for the Group had eighteen members with periods of theological training that varied from five years to none ; and these members had a loyalty both to the

Parish and to their own traditions, for they represented eight major denominations which, through them, were co-operating at the complex grass-roots level. They were Baptists, Brethren, Congregationalists, Episcopalians, Reformed, Methodists, Mennonites, Presbyterians. It was a triumph that they worked so well together. It was a victory in the realm of inter-church co-operation beside which many other ecumenical achievements pale into insignificance.

Yet because it was a victory in a real-life situation, it reaped not just the riches from eight Christian traditions, it also reaped the tensions which their differences produced. It was one thing to discuss techniques and strategy and programmes. It was quite another thing to tackle problems which challenged members' deepest beliefs, for that could add intolerable tensions to the many that were already borne. There was value in that irritant process which challenged complacency and inspired creative action. But it was all too easy for the irritant process to develop into a corrosive agent which brought not inspiration but destruction.

And so, almost unconsciously, doctrinal differences were driven underground. A theological truce was observed. With a few dramatic and painful exceptions, the deepest issues of the faith were avoided. It just did not seem to be worth it.

'And this was tragedy,' as a pastor says today. For the avoidance of ' mere theology ' was the avoidance of the ' mere ' knowledge of God's will which in practice determined whether or not lay members had an equal say with pastors, whether time should be given to prayer or politics or both, and whether men should put their trust in blueprints and committees or in Jesus Christ. It was tragedy, in other words, because the questions which were submerged were precisely those which called for the most urgent attention—the place of the laity, the nature of the Church, the Person of Jesus Christ: these were the pillars on which the work of the Parish should stand. And although to evade them was to bypass serious conflict, it was also to bypass any chance of the Parish finding real maturity.

But the bypass was taken. And it led to an almost unobserved change in the Group's reason for existence, a change which could drain the Gospel out of their work and out of the church as well. For it led to a concentration on the kind of ministry which raised no obvious tensions; to a courageous and thoughtless activism, a dehumanising realm which served men more than it loved them; to the giving of the life of the staff in necessary, costly, and superficial service; to the galvanising of the church into action instead of to helping its members come alive with the life of Christ.

The aim of the Group had been to build a church which would reflect the wholeness of the Gospel, and which would bring that wholeness into the lives of broken men. It looked as though they might build an institution which would reflect their own divisions, and which would bring still more confusion to already confused, divided men.

One night in 1955 a Group Ministry meeting failed to avoid the areas of deep disagreement. The members were dispersing in a gloomy atmosphere. 'What's new?' asked a late arrival, looking at his friend's dejected face. 'Nothing's new,' came the strained reply. 'Except the Group's falling apart. . . .'

A fatal midnight car smash on First Avenue was the tragedy
which shocked the Group into coping with the failures they
describe. But this creative disaster was preceded by a series of
events, some pedestrian, some painful, but all pressing the
staff towards the one valid solution. We cannot say how
these events affected every staff member; but at least we may
glimpse something of their impact on one or two of those
most deeply involved.

Each member knew that the riddle could not be solved
merely by organisation, by new techniques, or by paper reso-
lutions. The problem went far deeper than that, for it affected
their whole attitude to one another and to their lay friends;
it affected their whole way of life. In other words, it was a
profoundly religious problem. It received a profoundly religious answer.

' During the early years,' says one of the Group, ' some of us
took the religious discipline very lightly. We were less concerned with worship than with activism. And the Bible, for
example, was mainly a springboard for riding your own pet
theological hobby-horse.' It was true that each member of
the Group had in his home the symbols of a pair of candle-
sticks, a cross, and an open Bible; but many did not use
the Bible regularly because, as they expressed it, ' in an
activistic enterprise such as the Parish it is impossible to give
large blocks of time to purely devotional reading.' It was
also true that most members honoured their pledge to attend
Group Ministry worship at nine a.m. on Sunday mornings;
but not every member came, and the worship often meant
very little to some of those who did. Even the monthly
retreats at the farm, which were occasionally times of real
spiritual renewal, were far more often days when the details
of policy and administration were thrashed out. At all events,
the religious discipline was at this time (1955) a ' discipline ' in
name only, for, as a Group report expressed it, ' there is no

check made and no disciplinary action is ever thought of:
for instance, no one knows whether or not other members of
the staff actually do follow the daily Bible readings.' And
when a friend from a Protestant community in France asked
gently, 'Is this liberty unto life, or liberty unto death?' most
(but not all) of the staff could only shrug their shoulders and
repeat, 'In an activistic enterprise such as this, it is impossible. . . .'

Right from the start, however, there were those whose
eyes were wide open to the need for a radical religious discipline which would be the mainspring of the whole life of the
Group. Typical of these was the gentle John Crist whose deep
sense of worship had matured immeasurably in long weeks
of pain during a serious illness in 1954; 'Pray for me,' he
wrote to 104th Street church from the hospital, 'that, as I
enter again into the confusion of the world, I may not forget
the things which God has taught me here.' He did not forget.
And it was partly through his quiet persistence that late in
1955 the staff decided to give half an hour to Group Bible
study before their fortnightly evening meetings.

Most came to these study groups tired after a long day's
work. Some found it hard not to spend the study time thinking of the issues which would arise in the business meeting
which followed. A handful had worked on the Bible passage
beforehand and were alive to the issues that it raised. 'But,'
says one of the ministers' wives, 'most of us were bored.' In
fact, one hard-working member was never able to stay awake
for the full thirty minutes; by degrees he would slump back
into his chair, his head would drop forward, and his open
Bible would lie limply on his lap; the best that could be said
on the positive side was that at least he snored softly.

Into this unpromising situation came a slight, intense, immaculate lawyer in the summer of 1956. William Stringfellow
was twenty-eight years of age, and he lived and worked with
the Group for eighteen months. Unlike the other members
who shared his profound concern, he made no allowance
whatever for the complex nature of the Parish workers' problems, he completely disregarded the feelings of those who
had worked there for eight years longer than he; and day

after day, week after week, he attacked without mercy those members of the Group who were neglecting the Word of God. He was rude, he was ruthless, he was rigid, and he was right.

One evening at a Bible study in the Crists' small apartment, most members of the staff were relaxing in chairs or on cushions on the floor; one was stretched full-length on a comfortable settee. Stringfellow was leading the group, and only two or three were taking part in the discussion. It soon became clear that few had done any preparatory work on the Scripture passage and fewer still were really interested in working on it now. When he failed to get an answer to a simple question on the subject matter, Stringfellow's microscopic reserve of patience vanished altogether, and he leaped to his feet and exploded at the Group:

' How dare you come here unprepared for Bible study? How dare you nod there in your chairs instead of listening to the Word of God! This is just an empty religious ritual. It's downright blasphemy!'

' Take it easy, Bill,' came John Crist's quiet voice.

' I will not take it easy: that's the last thing I'll do. I'm protesting that the Group is guilty of taking worship easy. It's not merely that you're not taking the Bible seriously. You're not taking *God* seriously!'

The addition of Stringfellow's intense attack to the strong, steady, patient pressure of such men as John Crist and Geoffrey Ainger (an English Methodist working with the Group) was beginning to have its effect. It was true that for some members the Bible studies continued to be, in Ainger's devastating words, ' a boring, innocuous, or, at best, an interesting burden '. But others were beginning to take their religious discipline more seriously. And some were suspecting that this discipline might hold the key to their own most pressing problems, especially the problem of their relationship with the laity. Geoffrey Ainger showed how the New Testament implied a relationship between St. Paul and his young churches very different from that between the Group and East Harlem's lay men and women. He introduced the staff to Roland Allen's shattering indictment, *Missionary Methods: St. Paul's Or Ours?*, and even the most conservative members were impressed by the gulf between the apostle's ways with the laity and their own.

Then came Hendrik Kraemer. Straight from retirement as Director of the Ecumenical Institute in Switzerland, the immensely learned Dutchman was giving a series of lectures at Union Theological Seminary, and he welcomed Webber's invitation to lead a retreat at the Parish farm. For some members of the Group, that November (1956) retreat meant nothing at all at the time. For others it was dramatic revelation. Standing with his back to the fire in the farmhouse living-room, Kraemer transported his listeners to distant Indonesia where he had worked for many years on the island of Bali. He told how he had discovered the Bible as a vivid revelation of God's ways of building a living church whose converts became leaders from the start. ' So unpractical God is,' he mused with a smile. ' So unwilling to take sensible precautions.' He had insisted that the infant church in Bali should discover from the Bible the secret of the early church's power and vitality, and that in the light of this secret it should make its own decisions about its hymns and music and architecture, and supremely about its doctrine and its choice of ministers. And when the church asked Kraemer to head a delegation to the island's ruler, he not only refused to lead ; he refused to go at all. ' The church was forced back not on the missionary but on the Lord. " And it grew in wisdom and stature, and in favour with God and man." The ministry,' he protested with more relevance than he knew, ' the ministry has burdened itself with an excess of power. And the church as a whole is tragically weak because it neglects its frozen assets—the laymen!'

As they drove back from the farm to East Harlem, many of the Group questioned the relevance of the situation on an Indonesian island to the situation on Manhattan. Others—a minority—saw Kraemer's point as the beginning of an answer to the problem of the pastor-Parish relationship. One or two began getting a bulletin, *Laity,* from the World Council of Churches. Others rediscovered for themselves, in the Biblical drama, the early church's vigorous insistence that its members —lay and clergy—were interdependent members of Christ's Body. And it all came out of the realm of theory and into the sphere of explosive reality when one minister member felt that the time was ripe to preach a series of sermons on 'The Church as the Body of Christ'.

Unknown to him, he had become pastor of his church in the teeth of strong lay opposition: many members had wanted another minister, but their wish was overruled by the Group, and the fact was not forgotten. 'We are all the Body of Christ,' the pastor insisted, unconscious of the fact that he was lighting a powder-keg fuse. 'So the work of the church is not just the work of the minister, but of every member of the Body. Every member must minister. Every member must be responsible. Every member, including the minister, has faults, and he needs the help of other members. The minister sometimes has to put the people right. And sometimes the people have to put the minister right.' The powder-keg burst after the service. 'So we need to put the minister right?' came an ominous growl from one member at the Church Council meeting. 'How come then we don't have no voice in this congregation?' 'I agree with that,' complained a husky Puerto Rican as the tension in the meeting mounted high. 'We hear all this preaching about the Body of Christ, about being responsible ; but, man, we don't have no voice!' The atmosphere had become electric as a large Negro leaped to his feet, his head nearly touching the low roof of the storefront church. 'That's true! Take you!' he thundered, pointing a great, accusing finger six inches from the pastor's nose. 'We never wanted you for our minister anyway!'

'We never wanted you. . . .' The Word of God had fallen on fertile soil. And such devastating eruptions forced the Group to take that Word more and more to heart, to question again their relationship with the laity, and to suspect that events were thrusting them towards a climax.

Next spring (1957) some of them felt the thrust growing stronger during the visit of an unlikely-looking revolutionary. Suzanne de Diétrich was a small, crippled Frenchwoman whose sombre dress and straight black hair made her an un-impressive sight until one saw the sparkle in her eyes. She spoke of Bible study as an engagement, as an event, as a divine-human encounter, as a trysting place with the living God ; the Bible, for her, was God speaking through the events of the past and tuning the ears of his disciples to hear him

speak through events today. With a sense of excitement,
more members of the Group turned hopefully to the Biblical
narrative, for in the light of their failures they realised (as
some of them had known from the start) that above all other
needs, they needed to hear God speaking to them, both
through the events in Scripture and through the events in the
street. They had not long to wait.

On Monday, March 4th 1957, the Group met for its regular
fortnightly evening in the Calverts' apartment. It had been
a difficult, demanding day, and it was not surprising that
relationships were strained. The half hour of Bible study
dragged on to an indeterminate end, and then came a long,
involved discussion over matters of property and personnel
in which hardly two members of the Group seemed to think
alike. This was not a typical meeting, although it expressed
many typical divisions. It broke up late in an atmosphere of
frustration. The members made their way down the stairs and
paused outside to carry on the fruitless argument which was
relieved for a moment by the quiet ' Peace!' of John Crist's
greeting as he and his wife, Dotty, climbed into their old
station wagon and drove off down the street.

The group on the deserted sidewalk turned again to the
problem of their differences, and one of them idly watched
the lights change from red to green as the station wagon
gathered speed to cross First Avenue. And then, in an instant,
the quiet of the night was shattered. There was an explosive
crash, the shrieking protest of torn steel on tarmac, and the
agonising scream of the other car's brakes. Then silence. . . .

Dotty Crist was lying in the wreckage, unconscious. So was
the driver of the other car who had tried to beat the lights.
But before his friends had raced the fifty yards to the tangle
of twisted steel, John Crist—the quiet man of God—was
dead.

' And that's how we were brought to our senses.' The
minister's wife who reached that sober conclusion did not
realise at the time all that John Crist's death would mean to
her. All she knew then was that she had been unspeakably
moved by the strange, symbolic way in which John's death
fulfilled his aim of identifying himself not only with East

Harlem but also with his Lord: ' This was the way that Christ had died; this quiet, patient, loving man had such a bloody, painful, public death.' All she knew at the crowded funeral service was the overwhelming fact that ' John was still part of Christ's Body; we were still linked to him; and we knew that we were the people of God, the Christian community in heaven and on earth.' And above all, at that service she knew, as she had not known before, the fact of the Resurrection, the reality of the presence of Christ in the midst of the congregation. All of which meant that through John's death she had been brought into a terrible and supremely real encounter with God.

Today each member of the Group speaks of John Crist's death with a sense of wonder and of indescribable thankfulness. The reason for their gratitude is that for many this event became the revelation which slashed through the superficial elements of life and left them with a sense of ultimate reality, a sense of what really mattered in their ministry; namely, *men,* for John Crist was a man; and *God,* for he had met them and renewed them in John's death.

' God meets us in events,' Suzanne de Diétrich had said a few days before the fateful event on First Avenue. ' He meets us in events in the Bible, and he meets us in events today.' In the months that followed, as one member puts it, the event of the Bible ' began to take hold on all our lives; it became a means of grace.' By the fall of 1958 the thirty-minute Bible study at the end of a heavy day had been replaced by an hour and a half first thing each Monday morning. This was a direct response to the Group's increasingly sharp sense of need; not so much the need for new techniques or better organisation, but the need for God himself. To be sure, they had all been aware of that need since they first went to East Harlem. But it was one thing to assert, as a newly ordained pastor, that God is one's first necessity. It was quite another thing to confess, out of the pain and the turmoil and involvement of ten crowded years, that one's paramount need was not love or understanding or theology or faith, but that first and last, without exception—in social action, political involvement, evangelism, and worship—one's only immediate, urgent need was for the living God himself. ' Our only hope,'

they wrote, ' is to live in the world by God's grace and to find
the meaning of our life in worship.'

Not that they always succeeded in their aim. The demands
of the Parish were so great. But at least they were on the
road ; and it was a road which led them straight to the place
where their dilemmas were resolved.

19. THE STEADY BEAT OF WINGS

It was March 1959, and the members of the Group were excited by the way in which their new form of Bible study had been leaping into life. For six months now they had started their working week with a ninety-minute study to which all came fully prepared; they had each read the Scripture passage, they had studied a Bible commentary or two, and they were aware of some of the practical issues which the chapter raised. The return of Letty Russell (a former staff member) from Harvard Divinity School with honours in Hebrew and Greek was reinforcing the technical competence of the Group. The devotional reading which others had crammed into their programme was giving a new historical and spiritual depth to the sessions. In fact, the Monday morning study was frequently a vital experience in which the members' attitude to some fundamental aspect of the faith was strengthened or re-born or radically changed.

Crucial, as it turned out, was the change which continued to develop in the conception of the place of the laity in the church. For over ten years the members of the Group had believed that lay members must ultimately share in all decisions: it was true that lay men and women now took a leading part in many aspects of church life, but, as we have seen, they had no say at all in such fundamental questions as the engagement of personnel and the use of funds. Now it looked as though belief might be fully expressed in practice, as a series of lively Bible studies drove home the crucial rôle that had been played by laymen in the early church.

Their studies of the Gospels had reminded them that it was Christ's specially trained apostles who did 'notable signs and wonders'; but the same studies had shown quite ruthlessly that while his 'full-time workers' betrayed and deserted and denied him, his 'part-time workers' carried his Cross, and laid him in the tomb, and were the first to whom he came when he was risen.

These facts were no more than symbols. But the symbols

came alive when they turned to the drama of the Acts of the Apostles which read like a blueprint answer to lay members' protests that there was no divine guarantee that paid workers would have special grace to make all key decisions. 'Who chose new pastors in the early church?' came the question at Group Bible study. And in the very first chapter of Acts there was the answer in the appointment of an apostle to replace Judas; it was seen that he was not elected by a secret session of the eleven apostles, but by a meeting of *the church*, by disciples who numbered ' about a hundred and twenty '. ' And who handled the finances?' they asked. The reply came in the down-to-earth sixth chapter of Acts (and the end of the fourth chapter, too) where the handling of money, and the vital things which money bought, was entrusted to seven laymen who were not chosen by the apostles at all but by ' the whole multitude ' of church members. ' Where then was the seat of ultimate authority? Who made top-level decisions?' The fifteenth chapter of Acts left the Group in no doubt at all. For it seemed that in about the year 50 the first formal Council that the church ever held consisted not only of apostles, nor yet of apostles and elders, but of ' apostles and elders, *with the whole church* '; and its decrees went out with the authority of ' the apostles and elders and *brethren* '. And since the decrees were concerned not with rummage sales and Sunday School picnics but with fundamental doctrine, the early church's ways pressed home the need for radical change in the Parish power structure.

The first Saturday in March was set aside for a Parish Council retreat to discuss that very question. And with that in mind, the Group Ministry gathered on the previous Monday evening in the Webbers' tenth-floor apartment on East 102nd Street. They were meeting for worship and for discussion of whether the Group was, in fact, usurping powers which belonged to the church as a whole. The passage for that week was read from the lectionary by Randy Hammond, 102nd Street's pastor. He stood up, ran a big hand through grey-flecked curly hair, and began reading the first chapter of Second Corinthians; it seemed as though Paul withheld his sabre-thrust until the very last verse. One member was thinking less of the reading than of whether or not he was guilty of high-handed action towards laymen whose faith was as strong or stronger than his own: he had come, for once, without having read the Bible passage and was tranquillised by the first twenty-three unremarkable verses. With the twenty-fourth, he was electrified. For Paul was calling on God to witness to the Christians at Corinth that *he* had never treated them as less than equals, or done injustice to the faith by which they stood: ' Not that we lord it over your faith; we work *with* you for your joy, for you stand firm in the faith.' ' Precisely!' exploded one minister. ' Our trouble is that we *are* lording it over the laity's faith. We're a colonial power group. We're always saying, " The people aren't yet ready for responsibility," and we continue to hold the reins.' ' And that means,' said a pastor's wife, ' that we are patronising people: we're not like Paul; we're working *for* people and not working *with* them.' The discussion revolved around the single luminous sentence, ' You stand firm in your faith ' —for, of course, it was by faith that the Parish had to stand, faith in Christ, and not faith in the Group. ' Maybe,' said Randy Hammond as the study came to a close, ' maybe we need to give up the name " Group Ministry " altogether. Perhaps the Group has had its day '; and after a long meditative pause, he rose to lead his friends in Holy Communion.

Seventeen heads bowed in silent prayer. On the table before the leader were set the loaf and the common cup, symbols of God's sacrifice for Group and laity alike. The silence was more complete than usual; thoughts were running deep that night. After a while the celebrant took up the sacramental words; the prayers, the confession, the consecration, the approach to the solemn climax, '. . . likewise, after supper, he took the cup; and, when he had given thanks, he gave it to them, saying, " Drink ye all of this; for this is my blood of the new covenant which is shed for you and for many. . . ."' ' And for many. . . .' The climax had come. The loaf was slowly passed around the circle, and a fragment broken off by each. Then the cup was raised and held high for a moment before it was passed from hand to hand. ' And for many. . . .' They were receiving the same gift that every local lay member had received—the ultimate gift, God's most precious gift, the gift of the life of Christ. The cup was returned to the leader who like his friends remained still for a long moment. Then the quiet was broken with the great prayer of Thanksgiving: '. . . and we heartily thank thee that thou hast assured us that we are very members incorporate in the mystical Body of thy Son, which is the blessed company of all faithful people. . . .' Silence once more. Silence that seemed to last a very long time while the Communion penetrated deep, as it were, into their minds and their hearts. Then down they went from the upper room and out into the night, thinking of those who were their comrades in the church, those other members of the Body of the Son, ' which is the blessed company of *all* faithful people. . .'

Saturday, March 7th 1959, dawned dull and cheerless and grey. Both laity and clergy on the Parish Council seemed unusually subdued as they climbed into three station wagons and began their journey to the farm.

At first, as they drove north on the Saw Mill River Parkway, they looked out on a hostile winter landscape, with its tawny fields and its snow in the hollows and at the foot of unfriendly trees. But by the time they turned on to the Taconic Parkway, the sky was clear and the air crisp and pure; and when the cars swung past a sunny meadow on to Peekskill Hollow Road, a gasp went up at the sight of the haze of pale green on the birch trees, and the signs of spring multiplied as they bumped along between the firs, past swollen brooks, and over the leaping waters of the Putnam Valley river. Two miles on and the white stone walls of the farm appeared between the trees, and the cars coasted down an incline before they came to a halt. Suddenly, as the engines stopped and the Council members opened the doors, the air was filled with a strange and marvellously rhythmic sound. All eyes turned to the hollow by the trees where a great flock of startled geese was rising from the old farm pond, and the clumsy thrashing of wings on water was changing to a confident beat. Rising high, they flew above the silent watchers and wheeled round in a great half-circle, hiding the sun for a moment like a cloud, before the steady beat of wings grew fainter as they headed north in perfect V-formation.

' We could learn from them, I guess,' a Councilman mused,

as he watched the united, single-minded flock make its way towards its goal.

By the time that lunch was over and the dishes washed and the yellow-topped tables all wiped down, the log fire in the main room was crackling away in the wide brick hearth. The Council members took their seats, and after Carlos Rodriguez, their lay chairman, had led them in prayer, he read the chapter for the week from the Parish lectionary: '. . . Not that we lord it over your faith; we work with you for your joy, for you stand firm in your faith.'

He put down the Bible in silence. For months some members of the Group had been discussing with laymen the possibility of giving all their powers to the church. Some laymen had said privately, ' If that should happen, then no one can say the age of miracles is past!' Now these same laymen were wondering if their scepticism would be justified. Carlos Rodriguez was speaking: ' I'll ask Randy to make a statement.'

The six-foot minister rose to his feet. He had been asked to speak for the Group, and now, standing beside the fire, he took the plunge. First he outlined the history of the Parish and spoke of the developing relationship between laity and staff. ' Originally,' he went on, ' the Group Ministry was comparable to an order of Roman Catholicism to which its members returned, with primary loyalty, for nurture and strength. This is not the ministry as we now understand it. The ministry is not the clergy. The work of the clergy, as Paul puts it, is " the equipment of *the saints* for the work of ministry ". In other words, the ministry is the work of every member of our churches: every member has a ministry as a Christian. And this means that it is improper to maintain an organisation known as the Group Ministry. It's out of date.'

And that essentially was that. There was discussion, of course. Some felt that Randy Hammond's proposal went a lot too far. But every member of the staff urged that the Group should cease to be the sole authority over personnel and finance, and that each and every policy decision should be taken by the church through its elected Parish Council, drawn from laity and staff.

Within minutes the verdict was made. The Group Ministry ceased to be a centre of power. All its authority was given to the church. Even the name ' Group Ministry ' was dropped. Not that its members were dropped. But their status as a special group was gone: now they were on the same level as the laity ; they had no more and no less power than the man in the pew.

This was more than petty church politics. It was the beginning of an answer, as we shall shortly see, to the Parish's deepest problems. But it was also a great act of faith. It was an act of faith on the part of a movement which for over ten years had been regarded by church leaders all over the country as a symbol of the way in which the inner-city break-through could be made. The Group Ministry had been instrumental in creating the church in the wilderness. It had inspired the emergence of similar churches in other city slums. It had fired the imaginations of men who had never even seen East Harlem to follow the same approach in countries over-seas. Now there was no ' Group Ministry ', no central body with power to give a clear-cut vigorous lead. Now there was just a church: a church which might disintegrate as each man went his own way ; or which might give new vision and strength as, together, all its members went God's way.

The Council broke up: some members talked together in groups. The chairman, Carlos Rodriguez, went out to enjoy the keen clear air and the silence by the pond. Far away to the north, no doubt, the single-minded flock still flew, keeping formation, holding course, bringing the promise of spring with the steady beat of wings.

20. LANDFALL

Yet the new beginning which had come to the Parish with the first sign of spring was seen by some dismayed church members as a deathblow to the church.

'Are you leaving?' one pastor was asked next day by an anxious parishioner. 'Is the Parish folding up?' It took a great deal of patience to explain again and again that the Parish was probably entering the most mature phase of its life to date; but the explanation began to make sense when it was learned that laity and clergy were to share responsibility for the whole of the church's life. 'Including personnel, Reverend?' 'Yes, including personnel and finance.'

Dismay was not confined to East Harlem. From all over the country letters poured into the Parish office, asking if the Group had been disbanded. Concern was most acute in the sister parishes in Chicago and in Cleveland. It was difficult to explain that the members of the staff were as devoted as ever to their work, that they had no intention of abandoning their disciplines, and at the same time to state that the Parish now had no 'Group Ministry' as such.

So when the four congregations had grasped the nature of the change, the Parish Council went on record as 'approving the use of the term " Group Ministry " again, with the clear understanding that the Group Ministry has no powers of decision in matters which affect the life of the Parish, the Parish churches, and members'.

Superficially, this was merely an administrative decision. But it was of first importance that in fact the decision was *religious* in character. It sprang directly from the deepening worship life of the Group, and especially from their rich Bible study sessions which had led them to share all their powers with the laity as a matter of obedience to God. So perhaps it was natural that such a decision held at its heart the beginning of an answer to the Group's fundamental problems: their failure to share real power with the laity, their tendency to be independent of the laity, and their failure to use their doctrinal differences as stepping-stones to God.

Clearly, the first had been answered. All power was to be shared with the laity. All decisions were to be made by the church as a whole. So when a new pastor was needed for one of the churches, the Parish Council appointed a committee of both laymen and clergy. The laymen had their own ideas about engaging personnel. Instead of interviewing the applicants in the Parish office, it was decided that each pastor should have a meal with two or three committee members, and should also spend a day with them, looking round the Parish. There were four applicants, and each involved several meetings ; but despite East Harlem's traditional impatience with committee meetings, each member of the committee appeared for every single interview because now, as a Councilman declares, ' we knew the staff wouldn't pull the weight '.

Their choice was a great success. And such experiences did more than relieve the Group of excessive responsibilities ; they bound all the members of the churches together in fulfilling their common ministry.

The answer to the second problem of being independent of the laity had also suddenly emerged. When the Parish Council returned to East Harlem, bringing the news of its crucial decision, the face of one of the ministers' wives was a picture of consternation. ' But what status have we?' she asked her husband. ' If there is no " Group Ministry ", what relationship have we to anything . . . except to our local church?' ' And that, as she says today, ' was precisely the point.' By this she means that by losing their relationship to any authoritative body except the local congregations, the staff had gained rather than lost ; for the only status they now had was the status which any man or woman might win by their devotion to God and to their neighbour. And this brought a marvellous freedom to focus life on what ultimately mattered ; that is, on God and on people.

So this lack of status, this nakedness of Group members, was a painful but also a profoundly rewarding experience, for, as they declare, it opened the eyes of those who had been blind to their own deep need for the laity.

Now that shared responsibilities had exposed them to their

lay friends, they saw how much their need for the laity went right down to the roots of their faith and life as Christians. Now they saw how much they needed the challenge of the woman who put $5 in the collection plate to help stop one of the churches from closing down, and then went home through the snow, with $2 in her purse, to wait four days for the next week's Welfare payment. Now they knew that they really needed the forgiveness of those parishioners who came to reassure the pastor whose failure to supervise a church canteen had been the cause (so he said) of four teenagers being shot. Above all, they realised how much they needed the lay members' zeal for the work of the church: they needed it, and more and more they got it; for, twelve months after the decision at the farm, one pastor could declare, 'Lay men and women are pushing us on matters of faith and witnessing and prayer. They believe in prayer, they believe in divine healing, they believe God speaks to them. This is the wisdom of the laity.' And the Group now learned to depend more on that wisdom, and in return, far more of their lay friends learned to depend on the Group; for when East Harlem's lay men and women knew that their help was needed by the staff, they also knew that they needed the staff's help too—and they were not ashamed to receive it. 'It's the receiving that hurts,' a parishioner had said some years before as he thought of his dependence on charity. Now, in a host of ways, the *staff* were receiving from the laity, and so the laity were far more free to receive from the staff.

Yet strange to say, not only were pastor-Parish relations revolutionised by the hand-over of power to the church, but the same event began to transform relationships within the Group itself; it did so through the impetus it gave to the enrichment of the religious discipline.

'Now that decisions were made elsewhere,' says Norm Eddy, 'the staff had more time for the religious discipline.' For months the staff had wanted to develop a deeper devotional life, for their first hesitant steps in that direction seemed to bear so much fruit. It was the early strengthening of their devotional discipline which had resulted in the transfer of power; but now that transfer itself gave them time to devote to a very much richer religious discipline. And time given in that direction helped them resolve their third basic problem, that of religious differences within the Group. It led to much more besides. It led to a new pattern in the lives of staff and laity alike. It led to a new era for the Parish. If John Crist's death had been the seed of new life, and if the farm decision was the first green shoot that showed, then the new religious discipline was the root that spread and multiplied and helped that new life to mature.

Three new decisions were made. They were made by the Group for the Group. But they were intended for each member of the church who felt the need for a Christian discipline; and slowly—very slowly—as the next few chapters show, that intention is being realised.

The decisions affected the conduct of each day, the conduct of the monthly retreats, and the conduct of the individual's vocation: together, they affected each member's relationship with all his neighbours and with God.

The Ordered Day was a principle which, in the words of Letty Russell, involved ' planning each day as an offering to God'. Every morning at 8.25 she leaves the tiny two-room apartment which she shares with Flossie Borgmann, and walks round the corner to 106th Street church (where she is pastor) for worship with others who share in her ministry there. ' It's a lot easier to get out of bed in the morning if you know there are others waiting for you.' A hymn is sung in the chapel, and then the Parish prayer of confession is said. After this the psalm for the day is read, and when the Gloria has been sung, the Scripture passage from the lectionary is used as a basis for meditation. Then comes ten minutes' silence. The silence is used ' to order the day ', to determine priorities and sketch out a rough plan of action. This is followed by ten minutes' intercession before the Benediction is asked. Without this discipline of daily worship and without this ordering of the day ' you cannot live ', says Letty Russell. ' Whether the spirit is willing or not, you worship and pray and study the Bible even if the house burns down: when you feel least like it, you need it most.' And the effect of this ordered day on the life of the Group was as decisive as the effect of the new retreats.

The Group Retreats at the farm had nearly always been

occasions for thrashing out policy, but now that all policy decisions were made elsewhere they became oases at which the Group members drank deep and were refreshed and re-directed. For twenty-four hours every month they lived to-gether and prayed together and discussed such questions as the meaning of Easter, the approach to East Harlem's youth, the meaning of Christian marriage, the heart of private and public worship. One early retreat was on the spiritual life: they used a classic by St. François de Sales ; all had studied it beforehand and so they were alive to the issues which were raised when Norm Eddy read it aloud at mealtimes. The day began with Holy Communion which was followed by an hour of meditation ; then came a session in which members' prob-lems about prayer were discussed. But most of the time was spent in silence, and that included the time of the closing evening service and the long drive home in the dark. ' Next morning,' says one of the pastors, ' we were a different group.' They were different because this retreat, like the ordering of the day, set action in the context of worship ; and that, as we shall shortly see, was a fact that impinged on every facet of their work and life. But there can be no doubt at all that the fruits of the retreats and of the ordered day would very soon have been left to rot had it not been for the last of the three innovations.

An Adviser for each member of the staff was the dynamic that brought the religious discipline alive. ' We need to put teeth into our disciplines,' one man had remarked as he reflected on his failures to appear at Sunday morning staff Communion. Another, who rarely fulfilled his pledge to pre-pare for the Bible studies, confessed, ' I'm told I ought to. I know I need to. I don't. And I need someone to help me.' In fact, being very human (or, as one pastor says, ' being unfaithful, irresponsible, and sinful '), each member of the Group needed an adviser whose task was not only to advise but also to check that pledges were actually being fulfilled. ' It's a gimmick, if you like,' a pastor's wife declares, ' but it's a gimmick that keeps the channels open to God's grace by making you do what you ought to do with your life.' Each member chose his own confidant ; most chose other Group members, but some chose a lay man or woman. They met privately once a month and would sometimes outline their

goals—religious and otherwise—for the next half year; and
thereafter, month by month, the results would be assessed.
'Are you reading the daily lectionary? Are you praying?
Are you ordering your day? Are you attending staff Communion? Have you made good your relationship with so-
and-so?' These were the kinds of question which each
member knew his adviser would ask him every month. And
this, says one pastor, 'is a very humbling and a very powerful
business, for there is a kind of inescapable honesty to which
one is driven when one must confess the inadequate way in
which one is fulfilling one's obligation to God.' And if it is a
humbling and powerful business, it is also a very painful
business; but, as the pastor concludes, 'Perhaps the very
painfulness of this relationship and the way in which we have
managed to avoid it at every opportunity indicate how really
necessary this is for our life in Christ.'

Necessary and enormously enriching it certainly proved to
be, because at last the religious discipline, which had been, for
some, little more than a pious intention, really *became* a
discipline; it became a discipline which began to penetrate
into every corner of their work on the street, in the homes, in
the courts, in the Parish churches. This meant that worship
was becoming the sinews and the muscle behind the whole
wide sweep of Parish life. And the result was that many painful problems began to lose their sting—not least that of the
Group's religious differences. For, as one pastor says, 'in an
atmosphere of worship, an unconscious determination to
depend on your own theology is often replaced by a conscious
effort to depend on God; and an absorbing concern with
yourself can be replaced by a concern for your Lord and for
your neighbour.' This meant, in Dibby Webber's words, that
'Where there were rigid personalities, we were now becoming
open to each other'; it meant that disagreements could often
be described as 'a healthy, therapeutic experience'; it meant
that it was becoming possible to face differences, to learn
from them, and even to make them a means of grace.

This radical religious revolution did more than give a divine
perspective to the Group's involvement in East Harlem's
hopes and struggles. On the deepest level, it began to weld
the Group and the laity into a united church, a church in

which those lay men and women whom Kraemer had called
' the church's frozen assets ' were thawing out, and gaining
new vision, and taking their rightful place beside the staff.

One evening in the autumn of 1959 a member of the Group
walked up 104th Street to call on his adviser. He climbed the
tenement stairs to the sixth floor and knocked on the door of
apartment 20. His adviser was a Puerto Rican member of
104th Street church ; he was a member of the laity. Sitting
over coffee at the kitchen table, the pastor first described his
failures and achievements in the last month, and then went on
to confess his inability to cope with the seemingly insoluble
problem which had dominated all his thoughts for a week.
The coffee cups were pushed aside ; they talked of their faith
and their lack of faith ; they thumbed through the Bible to see
how those who had gone before them won through. And
then they prayed. The layman prayed first. It was a prayer so
simple and real and honest that it cut through the tangled
jungle of confusion and opened up the problem and the pastor
to the light of God. And when the prayer was done, there was
silence in the kitchen, except for the ticking of the cheap
alarm clock. The pastor's head was bowed and still. It was
his turn to pray ; but he simply said, ' Amen.' For, in fact, no
more praying was required. He had been given all he needed
through his friend.

So the church—and not merely the Group—moved slowly
towards maturity in the strength of the new disciplines which
were the last stage on one pilgrimage and the first stage on the
next.

PART SIX

THE DIVINE GUARANTEE

21. THE NEED TO BE BURIED ALIVE

At the start of 1960 the news from East Harlem's sister Parishes was good. In Chicago the West Side Christian Parish now had three storefront churches with a multi-racial membership of about two hundred. The Inner-City Protestant Parish in Cleveland had grown from two churches to six by attracting four already existing congregations—Evangelical and Reformed, Baptist, Episcopalian—to its membership and aims. Across the Atlantic, British pastors who had worked with the Parish were starting similar work in Glasgow and in London.

In East Harlem itself the life of the Parish's four hundred and fifty communicant members was still based on three storefronts and one regular (Presbyterian) church; but their plans for the future ranged from the building of a small permanent church in the centre of the district to the forming of small congregations whose worship and service would centre in the homes of Parish members.

But as so often in the past, most members' concern went much deeper than buildings and methods to the constant need to become more effective disciples of Christ in the world. This general concern was expressed at the 1960 New Year service in 100th Street church:

'How can we reach full maturity as a Parish? Does God guarantee a clear-cut way?' The preacher looked enquiringly round the crowded congregation. 'Yes, he does. Right here in St. John's twelfth chapter. "You must be buried alive," Christ says. "Like a grain of wheat." Unless it's buried, he declares, it just doesn't grow; it lies on the surface, wrapped up in itself; and life passes it by. Yet once it's buried . . . *then* it can take root and come alive and mature and bear

fruit. But only if it's buried. . . .' The pastor looked round the
packed pews again: ' That's the choice. We can live on the
surface: we can close our doors on the fouled-up lives of
those around us, and keep clean as we wither away and die.
Or we can follow Christ, and bury ourselves deep in the dirt
of a world that is needy and sinful and terribly real ; and then
at last we can take root and live and mature and bear fruit.
This was Christ's way. And he says it's our way too ; the way
that leads to suffering and death and burial ; the way of incarnation, the way of crucifixion—the one way with God's
guarantee that it leads to a real resurrection.'

Back in 1948 when the three young pastors had first come
to East Harlem, they slowly became convinced that the only
valid form of mission was one that would follow the way God
took on the first Christmas Day when he gave the world not
his good advice but his only Son. ' And his name shall be
called Emmanuel, which being interpreted is, God with us.'
Their task, they believed, was to be *with* men in such a total
way that their whole lives would be identified with those of
their neighbours. Their aim was the aim of pastors everywhere: to help bring Christ's resurrection life into the ordinary world. And, looking back on the years of their ministry,
it seems that the new life which the Parish is bringing to East
Harlem is appearing only as ministers and laity follow this
way of ' incarnation ' which at times is also a way of ' crucifixion '. The Parish staff would reject this language as arro-
gant and presumptuous ; they would protest that it likens their
work to that of Christ himself. And yet the events which these
last chapters will describe seem to show that their ministry
has followed, at least symbolically, the hard way that Christ
took from Christmas Day to Easter Sunday: the way that
he passed on to his Church in the plain command, ' Follow
me!'

Of course they could not repeat the Incarnation ; for ' We are
sinful individuals,' they said. So they did not even dream of
describing their ministry as one of ' incarnation '. Even the
word ' identification ' was eventually rejected. This was because, however much they wanted to do so, it was impossible
for college graduates to identify themselves completely with
their East Harlem neighbours. They could limit their friend-

ships to people in the district, they could send their children
to the local schools, they could live on a much lower salary
than they would have earned elsewhere; but although this
affected almost everything they did (including the price they
could afford to pay for groceries), it could not affect the more
basic fact that while most of their parishioners were trapped
in the district, they themselves could leave any time they chose
and find satisfying work at much better pay. The fact that
they might never choose to leave was of little importance.
What mattered was that they *could* leave. And they knew it.
And so did their neighbours.

This fact alone was a bar to complete identification of their
lives with those of other residents. So, in seeking a word
which might symbolise their attempts to follow the way of
Christ, they rejected 'identification' and chose 'participation'. For them, this had a much less patronising sound.
'*Christ* identified himself with men,' they said; 'but we stand
on different ground from him. He humbled himself. We can't.
There is no lower place for us to go.'

So they participated as fully as they could in the whole life
of East Harlem, and as the years raced by they lost the
strained self-consciousness which had marred their early
efforts to find common ground with their neighbours. They
lost their embarrassment at being college-bred: 'I'm the
only college graduate on this block,' said one of them with a
laugh, 'and I'm mighty proud of the fact!' This was just the
attitude that most parishioners would have had if they had
been to college; it meant that the speaker was participating
freely in the life and thought of the district. This conquest of
a superficial effort to 'belong' was even seen in the clothes
the staff wore. They gave away the working slacks and canvas
jackets which might have narrowed the gulf between them and
the many local people who were poorly dressed, for in fact it
looked like play-acting, and it broadened the gulf instead.
They began wearing 'ordinary' suits, for it seemed that to
take their neighbours seriously meant that they had to be
themselves, and for most of them the wearing of suits was a
part of being themselves. It was only as 'themselves' that
their lives became so deeply intertwined with the lives of those
about them, that when they were asked, 'Why don't you
leave?' they were shocked and replied, in blank surprise,

'Leave? Why? East Harlem is home.' And they remembered a Parish worker's poem:

Cement is not green yielding grass,
Nor do crows nest in brick.
From my window there is no hill to rest my eyes,
No melting field,
No small white birch
To shine with sun or rain or ice.
No rabbit darts from the hedge to halt
trembling at my footfall.
My feet do not crush fragrant wintergreen.
My face is greeted by no hemlock's brush. . . .

And these are things of home.
In these my soul was cradled, succoured, raised.
To these my heart responds as life to life.
As much necessity as food and drink.

Yet here . . . here I am happy. Why?

I see the wind in tossing lines of clothes,
The sunset glow in roseate window banks.
The rain is music on the roof and eaves.
Gushing gutters bring the sky to earth—
A roof at night hangs between two star-filled heavens. . . .

But, supremely . . . the people. . . .

From a lonely tower with a view
one can feed one's soul to satiety.
Here need knocks
        and asks
            and in the asking gives
For God is not indeed
        in wind
            nor rain
                nor earthquake
but in the still small voice of someone's need.

So the Parish workers' lives were woven so deeply into the

texture of East Harlem that when Buffy Calvert, the writer of the poem, was asked about the sacrifices she had made, her reply took the form of a protest:

' I have made *no* sacrifice! I'm enormously grateful for the chance to work among neighbours who have so much to teach me about life and with whom I know the beginnings of a fruitful sharing of the life in Christ. I cannot tell you how much my years here have meant to me. . . .'

' But what about your children?'

' Our children have found that New York is a very stimulating and exciting place in which to live and grow. And they are particularly blessed by the fact that they have the opportunity to experience naturally as the they grow up the reality that all men are brothers regardless of race or creed or station in life. Theirs is a unique and wonderful freedom: that of being truly at home with all manner of men and women.'

' But what of the dangers?' the questioner persisted.

' Our children are *safer* in East Harlem than in a suburban compound,' came the firm reply. ' Here they are exposed to the whole of life—the good as well as the bad. When they see the drunks who visit our apartment, they learn to beware of drink. When they meet young addicts in the local schools, they see what drugs can do and they learn to keep off narcotics.'

' The lesson we all learn,' her husband added, ' is that in separation there is no security.'

The security which they and their children and their parishioners were building was a security based not on separation but on participation, on exposure to one another, on sharing the whole of life with one another.

This ' way of participation ' was the strong way which broke down barriers and which proved itself by forging friendships that sometimes erupted in overwhelming demonstrations of affection. When one pastor and his wife returned to their church after two months' absence in the South, it seemed as though half the block turned out to give them a wildly enthusiastic welcome. Crowds of Puerto Ricans, Negroes, and Italians, churchgoers, non-churchgoers, drug addicts, storekeepers, and hordes of children, swarmed round the entrance to their tenement, shouting, whistling, laughing, and shaking their hands until they finally reached their door and embraced the last one of their friends, who looked at the pastor and smiled as he confessed, ' Gee, man ; we wondered was you really coming back.'

Far more important than the staff's participation in the life of East Harlem was the fact that more lay people than ever before were participating in the drive to meet the district's urgent needs. Dramatic large-scale involvement in the problems of narcotics, gang warfare, and racketeer landlords was being inspired by the laity and largely carried through by them. But at least as important was the undramatic, unobtrusive concern for those in need which was shown by many men and women whose horizons had only recently been confined to the walls of their apartments.

There was Mrs. Jones, who had said as she shut the door in the visiting pastor's face, ' I don't want to bother nobody and I don't want nobody to bother me.' A few years later, as a newly enrolled church member, she was preparing food each day for an elderly neighbour who could not take care of himself ; and four years later she was still ' bothering ' with him each day. There were Mr. and Mrs. Robinson, who a few years back left their apartment only one evening a month to visit friends in the Bronx ; now they had joined the Parish and were spending three evenings every week sitting and talking with lonely young addicts who wanted friends almost as much as they wanted drugs. And there was Felix Rodriguez, who had lived on 100th Street since 1941: ' I'd held down my job ; I went to the ball games ; for the rest, I kept mostly to myself.' Now, as a Parish Councilman, he spoke, when pressed, of the new concern he had for his neighbour: ' There was a fellow on my job. Nobody liked him ; and he didn't like anybody either. He was taken ill and rushed to the hospital. So I took up a collection just to show that the fellows cared about him, and took him a tin of tobacco and a pipe. Well, he came back to work and I won't say he's a changed individual, but he told me how much he appreciated the fellows caring for him. Since then his relationship with us seems much better. You sometimes even see him smiling now!'

Making meals for elderly men, befriending addicts and taking gifts to the sick were not the kind of things which

made the headlines. But they were the kind of thing which
Christ described as of the essence of his kingdom: ' I was
hungry and you gave me food ; I was a stranger and you took
me in ; I was sick and you visited me . . .'; they were the
kind of thing which neither Mrs. Jones nor the Robinsons
nor Felix Rodriguez would have thought of doing before they
joined the church ; and they were the kind of serious participation in the life of the community which built bridges and
bored tunnels and opened doors between the world and the
church.

Such individual acts went hand in hand with the work of
groups of church members. A handful of lay men and women
who had been moved from old tenements to a nearby housing
project began calling on their neighbours with the object of
forming a group to deal with the problems of new tenants.
Cockroaches were their first concern. And if there was one
thing that proved the contention that ' in separation there is
no security ', that one thing was cockroaches. Before the group
was formed, the exterminator man had responded to individual complaints and had fumigated single apartments : when
this happened, the cockroaches moved next door—and came
back again next day. But when the group of neighbours
arranged for all their homes to be dealt with at the same time,
the result was disaster for the cockroaches and a celebration
party for the tenants. This group met regularly, week after
week ; a real sense of comradeship gradually grew ; and soon
' You could tell that things were really happening because
people began to smile and talk in the elevator, instead of
standing in dead silence.' The group discussed schooling, the
need for more police patrolmen, and other questions, most of
which bore fruit in action. And after a while they moved
from cockroaches to Christianity by starting a regular session
for Bible study and prayer. Over a period of six months the
cold, impersonal project atmosphere changed ; solid social
improvements on a minor scale were achieved ; each member
of the group made lasting friendships ; and some of them
joined the church.

So as laity and clergy tried to follow the down-to-earth
way of Christ by participating in East Harlem's need for food
and friendship and pest relief and God, they began to build

a road for their neighbours which ran in the same direction Christ's first ' road' had done: not from the church to an alien world but from the world to the church.

But if ' participation' were to mean no more than social involvement, it would have been a plain betrayal of the church's ministry. If men's lives were to be made whole, and if they were to learn to serve their neighbours, they needed more than participation in the life of the world; they needed to participate in the life of the church.

To such men as Al Sand, a middle-aged laundryman, the church gave vision and strength because unlike East Harlem's disintegrating society, its members—dock workers, housewives, ministers—were a united team; united by their loyalty to God and to one another. Each member mattered, for each had his own special gift: gifts of running the Credit Union, the Sunday School, the office; gifts of preaching, counselling, serving on Christian Action. Al Sand knew that all these gifts together expressed the unity of the church's life. And he learned that this unity reached out to other inner-city churches whose workers visited East Harlem, to congregations across the land who were linked with the Parish by their prayers and their gifts, and to the church far overseas whose leaders sometimes came and worshipped in his church. All this gave depth and meaning to Al's life; it gave strength and purpose, too.

' It was through the example of the members and through Bible study that I learned to *do* things for people,' he says. Participation in the life of the church meant that Al Sand slowly became the kind of man who could participate creatively not just in the church but in the world. Alone, he had seemed devoid of gifts: in the comradeship of the church his gifts appeared. And although at first they were small and frail, they soon grew strong with exercise until he was working three nights a week with a local teenage gang.

So Al Sand's life was changed. And such a change inspired hope in others out beyond the church; for they were faced not with four hundred and fifty individual Al Sands but with four hundred and fifty united members of an impressive family. It was impressive because it had something more than different ideas from others ; it had different loyalties and different goals and a different way of life. And it was hard to ignore such a family, for it could not only be heard on the street ; it could be seen and judged and maybe admired. And it could be joined.

' And yet,' says one pastor, ' we can participate in the life of the world and of the church, and still be fundamentally useless to both. We can preach the Gospel and work like mad on social action projects, and remain self-centred, ruthless creatures whose good works leave men worse off than before.' Participation in the life of the world and church were vital: both were commanded by Christ. But if the Parish was to affect the roots as well as the fruits of society, it needed a higher participation: participation in the life of God.

Normally, this ' higher participation ' came through the worship and service of the church. It had not always done so. For in the Parish's early days, men's need for God himself had sometimes been obscured by their more obvious poverty: ' Initially,' the Parish wrote, ' we were appalled by the social evils of East Harlem and it seemed enough to undertake social action. . . .' But soon it became clear that church workers had to offer men not only their service but themselves ; what was needed, they declared, was ' our presence in the Parish, beside a boy in the courtroom, on the block when a fight starts, in our apartments with an open door when there is a need '. But even this self-giving proved inadequate: ' Standing alongside the men and women of East Harlem, face to face with hopelessness and tragedy,' they wrote, ' we realised that there was no way out by dependence on our solutions, or even on our faithfulness, but only on the faithfulness of God. East Harlem will not be helped,' they concluded, ' unless Jesus Christ goes through it, through men, through us too.'

' Without me you can do nothing,' they read in St. John's Gospel. But as a matter of fact it was perfectly plain that without Christ they could do a great deal. They could follow the hard road of ' participation in the life of the world ', sharing their neighbours' tensions and striving to bear their burdens ; and all this, they realised from long experience, could result in precisely nothing. They could follow the road of 'participation in the life of the church', calling on strangers, leading discussion groups, visiting the sick, giving men their counsel; and all this could foster the illusion that *they* were able to meet men's basic needs, it could focus men's faith on ministers and laity, and in the end, result in nothing. The fact that emerged was that fundamentally East Harlem needed more than Christians and the Christian church. It needed Christ. Christians and the church might offer men no more than their own ideas, their visions, their strength, their little kingdom; there was no guarantee that they would offer men Christ. But it was only when this supreme need was met that people in East Harlem were changed from the top of their minds right down to the bottom of their hearts.

It was so with Ben, a local drunkard, of whom a cynic once remarked, 'He'll need to come face to face with Jesus Christ before *he* changes.' Ben came face to face with Christ at a Sunday morning service, and afterwards he said, 'You were right, Reverend, about Christ meeting folks in worship. He was there today.' That was the point at which the higher participation began for Ben. It has not yet cured him completely of his habit, but it is slowly making him a good husband and father and neighbour.

This ultimate participation in the life of God brought big demands. It did not excuse men from responsible church membership; instead, it sharpened their desire to participate in the church's life. Nor did it excuse them from costly social action, which was clearly Christ's unavoidable command. But it did mean that whether in the church or in the world, they knew that their first need was to be men of faith, men whose involvement in the world did not mean entanglement in the world, men whose lives were conditioned not by the world but by God and the Gospel.

And yet this higher participation brought more than demands. It gradually gathered up the loose strands of men's lives and wove them together into a strong, meaningful unity. And those outside the church whose world was being atomised looked with hope to a community of 'ordinary' men whose life was no different from their own, except that it was not fragmenting but was becoming whole.

So the Parish members sought—as they seek today—to follow this way of participation in the life of God, in the life of the church, in the life of the everyday world. It was a way that sometimes took them through a Garden of Gethsemane, with its darkness and confusion and its ' Let this cup pass from me '. It was a way that sometimes brought them to a cross.

22. CRUCIFIXION

'Out of sixteen kids who were in my Youth Group ten years ago, seven are addicts and one is dead through using drugs.' The pastor was not criticising the youths. He was confessing his failure and expressing his grief; he was speaking indirectly of the cross his ministry entailed.

For ten years, with the laymen in his church, he had stood alongside these youths, trying to sort out their problems, praying for them, finding them jobs, helping to make their lives whole. But slowly those lives had fallen apart and finally succumbed to the power of heroin, leaving young men who had once been gay and alert and optimistic now sitting listless in a corner of a candy store, their eyes glazed and heads nodding like helpless, mechanical dolls. And those who had worked, year in and year out, to help preserve those lives and make them strong knew what Paul meant when he said, 'We are partakers in the sufferings of Christ'; for it was an agonising experience to watch one's friends descend into a living hell.

We must face the grim fact of addiction because it highlights the problems of society far beyond East Harlem, for 'we are the addicted society,' says a Parish pastor, encompassing the whole of New York City with a sweep of his arm, 'we are hopelessly trapped and diseased by whatever our dope may be. This is what life is without Jesus Christ. We are all addicts inside. In the heroin victim it's written large for the world to see. In me it's hidden. . . .' In other words, if there is an answer to addiction, there is hope for the rest of us too. And we must face the horror of addiction because it underlines the fact that the church must suffer and be crucified with those it seeks to serve; and that it must keep on being crucified even though the nails bite deep and the hope of resurrection is obscure.

The descent into 'hell' began at the age of fourteen for one of the pastor's sixteen boys. We may call him Raymond Johnson,[1] an alert, strongly built Negro, with a scar from a

[1] The names of all addicts have been changed.

knife fight creasing one ebony cheek. Dressed in his tartan shirt and tight grey slacks, he was laughing with his friends as they walked home from school when a car pulled up beside them, and a man offered them 'some stuff that will make you feel real good'. In a dark tenement hallway on that sultry summer day, Ray sniffed the white powder up his nose and experienced the indescribable sensation that heroin provides. A few weeks later this method ceased to satisfy, and he began dissolving the powder in water and giving himself skin injections. On his fifteenth birthday his family gave him a total of $4 in presents, and with this he stepped on to the last downward slope. He bought a 'mansize shot' of the drug and went up on the rooftop in the evening: there he fastened a borrowed hypodermic needle on to the sharpened end of a glass eye-dropper, and then pulled back the sleeve of his coat, drew the heroin solution into the makeshift syringe, and injected the drug into a vein. Now he was a 'main-liner'. Now he experienced all that heroin had to offer. Now he escaped the frustration which had made him seek fulfilment in drugs: his poverty-stricken home; his meagre schooling; his coal-black skin which set him apart and denied him a fair chance of a job. All these humiliations were gone. For now he was relaxed, he was supremely confident, without a care in the world. Life was good; life was big; and although eight years were to pass before he died, life was virtually over.

Ray Johnson was not to know about the chemical changes that heroin was causing in his blood, changes that were making him physically dependent on the harmless-looking drug. He was not to know that the powder was becoming almost as essential for him as water was to non-addicted people. But he very soon knew in practice what these grim facts involved: he knew that he was 'hooked', that he must have the drug or endure sheer agony. 'Early in the morning,' says an East Harlem resident, 'a car comes by and folks line up to get the stuff: but when the car doesn't come by they almost go crazy.' One day the car did not come by for Ray. He had been on heroin for a month (borrowing or stealing his $4 a day) and his need for the drug was acute. All day he wandered round the neighbourhood, looking like a wraith, for by now he was thin and dirty and hollow-cheeked.

By nightfall he was near-demented; he had a high fever and was racked by fits of vomiting and cramp-like stomach pains. 'Then,' as he put it, 'then came my saviour.' His 'saviour' was a man with a friendly grin and a small white packet of powder, and in minutes Ray was living in another, glorious world whose gay, high-hearted splendour seemed as though it must last forever. It lasted until the next morning when once more the car did not come by . . .

'Think of Jesus hanging on the Cross,' a young addict's mother said to a Parish congregation. 'Remember how he shouted out, "My God, why have you forsaken me?" Well, that's understood by the addict. . . .' This mother understood the cry as well, for she had suffered with her son. Ray's pastor and his lay church friends also understood the cry, for they were suffering with him. They were suffering because 'participation in East Harlem's life' meant that Ray Johnson was not 'a case', nor an object to be pitied, but a friend to whom they *belonged,* with whose life their lives were interwoven, and that therefore this disaster had happened to them as well as to him. Their pain was the pain of the helpless father watching his child's long agony as it dies from an incurable disease; it was the pain of Mary, watching her Son as he was crucified—' and a sword shall pierce thy soul also '.

Ray knew that some Parish members felt this way about him. He knew that although the church seemed powerless to help him, yet there were those in the church who lay awake at night because of him; and sometimes this made a difference. It meant, in a strange way, that somehow—only sometimes—he felt stronger because they were suffering with him. And he had need of all the strength he could get as his body cried out for yet more heroin until he felt like a frightened child with no way of escape.

He had good reason to be frightened. He was afraid that any day he might not get the drug he craved. He was afraid of being caught and sent to jail where he would not get it either. Most of all, he was afraid of the pusher who could torture him by withholding the powder, or could kill him any time he chose by giving him an overdose. Ray was trapped; and he knew it. He was trapped by the curse of addiction and by the unavoidable life of crime into which it had finally pulled him.

His daily needs had risen from one shot to two ; and then to three or four. His mother could no longer stop him from stealing by paying for the heroin herself (' I sure felt bad when she took her wedding ring off her finger and gave it me to sell '). Now he needed $12 to $16 a day: over $5,000 a year. To make $5,000 he had to steal goods worth four times that amount: $20,000 a year. And although, like most of the city's twenty-three thousand addicts, he was a shy, considerate, gentle person, his craving was sometimes so intense that it drove him all the way to violence, and he would hardly know what he was doing when he struck down a man or a woman on the street and raced off with a wallet or a purse.

All of his life was now a relentless search for the powder that could kill the pain of living for a few hours at a time. He was in and out of jail for theft or for possession of drugs. His pastor found him jobs out of town, but always he returned to the city and heroin. Once his friends in the Parish got him to Riverside Hospital which had beds for a fraction of the city's adolescent addicts. He took the withdrawal treatment, and when he came out, he kept off heroin for four weeks ; but those four weeks were bleak and meaningless, for he could find no real substitute for the deep satisfaction of drugs. At the same time he was terrified of becoming addicted once more: ' If I get hooked again,' he said to a friend, ' I'm gonna get an overdose.' He looked down as he spoke, nodding slowly as though he had made a discovery. ' That's it,' he said softly. ' That's the only way out for an addict.'

In fact, his way out was not so easy. For when those four brave weeks ended with a syringe on a rooftop at night, he did not use an overdose but, by mistake, he used a dirty needle. The result was a cellulitis which he tried hard to hide. But a few days later he was at the Parish medical clinic with an acute abscess in his arm, his face badly swollen, unable to eat, and the agonising swelling swiftly spreading. They rushed him to hospital where for two days he lay racked with pain. And then, without a fight—as though it didn't really matter—his head sagged sideways, and the pastor by his bed knew he was dead.

' He was one of the products of our church youth group,' said a Parish Councilman. And then he looked down, trying to hide his emotion: 'He never lived, you know. He never really lived. . . ."

It was a likeable, broad-shouldered Puerto Rican who back in 1956 had inspired the Parish to begin its fight against addiction—a fight that was to take it from East Harlem's streets to authorities in hospitals and jails and City Hall, and finally to testify before the President's Committee on Narcotics. Louis Leon, otherwise known as Pee-Wee, was a twenty-year-old member of 100th Street church. He had grown up in East Harlem and was one of three boys in a class of thirty-six who did not end up in jail or hospital as drug addicts: he had seen the terror and the tragedy which came to the thirty-three and to their families, and his response to the central Parish Purpose—' To set at liberty those that are oppressed '—was ' Let's set the addict free!'

Pee-Wee knew that in 1951 the Parish had dramatised the evils of addiction in a play called *Dope* which was seen by thousands on five different vacant lots ; he knew that since then a steady stream of addicts had sought help from the Parish ; and he knew that although his pastor, Norm Eddy, had worked with a hundred such people, only one of them had ceased to use the drug in the last five years. It was not a case of ninety-nine sheep in the fold, and one in the wilderness ; there was only a single sheep in the fold, and ninety-nine were lost.

So throughout the summer of 1956 Pee-Wee's massive figure, in cloth cap and leather jacket, could be seen on 100th Street, moving purposefully through the crowds, intent on his ' hopeless ' ministry. Before long a great many addicts were confiding in the young man with the lined face who had lived beside their problem all his life. He talked with them on the street and in the stores ; he had them home to meet his wife and his young children ; and gradually he realised that apart from the comradeship of the church (which very few indeed would accept), he himself had nothing whatever to offer them except his friendship and concern. He could advise the addict under twenty-one to apply for treatment at the city's 150-bed Riverside Hospital: it was true that few were willing to go ; it was also true that those who were willing were often jailed as drug offenders while waiting for admission. But at least the little hospital was there. For the adult addict New York State had no public hospital at all. When Pee-Wee tried to find help for those adults who wanted to fight their addiction, he discovered that, for the entire nation's fifty thousand heroin victims, there were only two hospitals and both were impossibly distant for most East Harlem men and women: in Lexington, Kentucky, and in Fort Worth, Texas.

At this point he turned to his pastor, Norm Eddy. Since coming to the Parish in 1949 Eddy had been appalled by the human problem of narcotics: some of his closest friends were addicts (and this was why he gave none of the details whatever for this chapter—' It would be unbearably painful to expose the suffering of one's friends '[1]), and so he responded eagerly to Pee-Wee's insistence that the Parish should not dodge the problem but should grapple with it realistically. Pee-Wee, who was Chairman of 100th Street Church Council put his case to the Parish in the autumn of 1956: ' We are better placed than anyone to tackle this problem because we're rooted right in the community and we can fight the battle where it is. And we know that we can count on the help of the people of East Harlem in the fight.' Soon Pee-Wee and Norm Eddy were working as a team based in a storefront on 103rd Street. Their aim was ' not only to save these men and women from their habit but to enlist their talents to build a Christian community where addiction would be impossible '.

The response was almost overwhelming. Forty-five people came to the first meeting for addicts and their friends. And in the first year over five hundred addicts sought help in the Narcotics Office. They entered beneath a sign which showed a glass syringe being smashed by a falling cross ; and inside, some of them discovered a little of what that cross signified. In the office they met not only sympathetic friends : they also met the church. For Norm Eddy and Pee-Wee had been joined in their task by volunteer workers from the Parish congregations—the parents of addicts, the friends of addicts, men and women who saw the need at first hand, and who responded to such appeals as that of a lay woman, Mrs.

[1] Quotations from Norman Eddy in this chapter are taken from Parish publications.

Tessie Bendter, as she stood before her friends in 104th Street church one Sunday: 'You with narcotics trouble in your family: you're probably ashamed. Don't be ashamed. There's no need to be ashamed of anything except of what we did to that man hanging on the Cross. Come to the Narcotics Office and learn how to handle the problem. Come tonight. You're *needed.*'

They came and they gradually learned that their very different gifts could all be used creatively. There was Carmen Cruzado, a slight, dark-haired, understanding Puerto Rican: her lively mind made her a first-class office manager who soon developed strong relations with the few other agencies working on addiction in the city. There were such people as Mrs. Bendter herself who knew many addicts well and who gave several nights a week, advising their families and listening with sympathy to the addicts themselves. And there were two former addicts with their costly gift of experience and their recent gift of faith: they were invaluable in the work of finding emergency food and shelter and clothes and jobs for addicts, and above all, in befriending them and standing by them in their need.

The pattern which developed in the fight was an all-embracing one: it reflected the church's conviction that God cares not just for souls but for people. There was the informal but serious research programme which Norm Eddy managed to fit in: studying the literature on narcotics, working on the medical side with the Parish nurse, and talking with patients and doctors at Riverside and Lexington hospitals, as well as with lawyers and Senators and Congressmen and more than a thousand addicted men and women and youths. There was the medical programme which showed addicts what help they might get from the city's slender hospital facilities; and with a local doctor in attendance, it provided its own treatment to withdraw the drug from the addict while he stayed at home. There was the educational programme at the Thursday night meeting for addicts, former addicts, and friends of addicts: here in the storefront office, talks were given by doctors, detectives, professors, narcotics users, and social workers with the aim of understanding the problem of addiction and of learning how to do something about it. And there was the pastoral programme which was run by two ministers and six laymen, some of whom were themselves former addicts: it provided religious discussions and retreats at the farm, and organised the Sunday Bible study; it also occupied countless hours of calling in hospitals, jails and homes in an effort to grapple with the addict's basic spiritual plight.

Slowly a community of addicts and former addicts and narcotics workers emerged, 'a community of acceptance', as one pastor put it, 'a community in which the addict is accepted not for what he can do but for himself'. And what, we may ask, did this community achieve? What were the results in terms of people?

There was Red Gomez, for one. He was a stocky, intelligent, middle-aged man who had once sat in a dreary prison chapel, listening with a few other addicts to Norm Eddy's Christmas sermon: '. . . the time that God came down into the world to be born among ordinary men. And the Gospel miracle is that God is waiting to be born in us—this Christmas. In you and me.' And as this tough, kindly man declared with childlike simplicity: 'It was then that I felt the birth of Christ in my heart.' When he came out of jail he was 'through with narcotics'. And despite the enticements of the drug racketeers, he is still off drugs today. He re-organised the Narcotics Recreation Centre, and was soon advising addicts' families and escorting young addicts to hospital. After eighteen months of church membership, he was serving on 100th Street Church Council, and on the Parish Council too.

But the achievement of Red Gomez was rare. It was true that apart from him there were several hundred addicts who had learned from the narcotics programme how to reduce their need for heroin and how to hold down regular jobs; it was true that many others had abstained altogether for average periods of six months; and it was also true that there were others besides Red who after two full years were still off heroin, still members of the church, and still working six days a week to help their addicted friends. But for every success story there were countless tales of defeat: for every Red Gomez, there were a hundred Tiny Scotts.

Tiny was another man who had been converted in jail and who came out and worked with the Narcotics Committee. He was a big jovial Negro with a happy-go-lucky air and a great gift for friendship with those who sought help from the Parish. One cold March night, when he had been off drugs for a year and a half, he was to receive the Commendation Card which was given every quarter to those who had success-fully abstained. Norm Eddy picked up Tiny's card from the office table, and glanced round the circle of addicts and narcotics workers before he said, ' On your behalf, I want to give this Commendation Card to our committeeman, Tiny Scott.' A chair scraped as Tiny rose to his feet. He hesitated uncertainly, then muttered as he made his way to the door, ' I don't want to accept till I get a few things straightened out. . . .' And the door let in a cold blast of air before it closed again behind him. Tiny had gone back on heroin. And those who had worked and worshipped with him, whose lives were intertwined with his, never saw him in the office again. All they heard of him was what he wrote after fighting for three long weeks to keep off heroin: when he lost yet one more fight, and the after-effects of the drug had left him utterly dejected, he wrote his terrible ' psalm ' and pushed it under Pee-Wee's door:

Heroin is my shepherd
I shall always want
It maketh me to lie down in gutters
It leadeth me beside still madness
It destroyeth my soul
It leadeth me in the paths of Hell for its name's sake
Yea, though I walk through the Valley of the Shadow of
    Death
I will fear no evil
For heroin art with me
My syringe and spike shall comfort me
Thou puttest me to shame in the presence of mine
    enemies
Thou anointest my head with madness
My cup runneth over with sorrow
Surely hate and evil shall follow me all the days of my
    life
And I will dwell in the house of misery and disgrace for
    ever.

It was at such times as this that those who had lived and worked alongside Tiny Scott felt that their ministry was almost unendurable. With Christ, on the night before Good Friday, they wanted to pray: ' Father, if it be possible, let this cup pass from me!' but of course it was not possible. The one way for Christ had been the way of the Cross. It was the one way for his followers, too.

The Parish Medical Clinic knew a little of this way of the Cross when in three painstaking years only ten of their several hundred patient-friends abstained from using drugs. Those involved in the pastoral programme knew something of crucifixion, too ; for in the same period, out of 1,200 addicts only twenty-five abstained, and only nine of these emerged to take part in the Parish programme: it was the fact that the remaining 1,175 were not only addicts but people— and very often personal friends—that made the result so very hard to bear. But they knew that unless they bore the result and the suffering that went with it, they would never come to grips with the addict's dilemma, and would never get beyond his cross to some kind of resurrection. ' In the crucifixion and resurrection of Christ,' wrote Norm Eddy from the Narcotics Office, ' the church claims to have the answer to life's riddles. Jesus chose certain suffering and death. He chose it because he knew it was God's will. And squirm though we may, we Christians cannot rid ourselves of this legacy. Each church in its own situation must accept its cross.'

This did not mean that the church must accept defeat. It meant that whatever the ' results ' might be, the church had to follow the way of Christ and realise that what looks like defeat to men is often God's strong prelude to triumph.

This was so in 1959 when ninety-eight per cent of addicts seen by the Parish in three full years were still selling their lives for little packets of white powder. And this was one reason why it was now perfectly plain that the way to fight this problem was not just the way of prayer and counselling and localised action, however ambitious that might be. It was a way that would open up hundreds of hospital beds to addicts, a way that called for a revolution at the highest level —in the medical profession, the City Administration, and the State Legislature.

' The doctors,' said Norm Eddy, ' with a tiny number of

exceptions, have done nothing whatever about the problem for over forty years'; he had found only three physicians who would consent to let an addict enter their consulting rooms; the only treatment adult addicts could get was at a few private hospitals—at $60 a day. Nearly half the prisoners in the city jails were addicts; their maintenance was costing twenty-five million dollars a year; New York was losing eighty million dollars a year in goods stolen to maintain the addicts' grim disease; and all the city could do, said the Parish, was 'to sweep the problem under the rug of indifference'. The law provided that in certain cases judges could commit addicts to hospital rather than to jail; but, in fact, there was no hospital in the entire state to which an adult addict could be sent. 'So when men and women come in off the street,' said Eddy, 'and we have to tell them there's no place they can go for treatment, we are for all intents and purposes saying, "Go out and steal, or commit prostitution, so you can get the drugs you must have."' In other words, society made it a crime for an addict to buy the drug he needed; and it made it almost impossible for him to overcome his need. The fact was, as Eddy insisted, that 'In the presence of a problem like addiction to narcotics, society hides its eyes. Conditioned as it is to success and progress, fearful as it is of unexplained human suffering, our society cannot face such facts as these. It chooses not to look.'

But the church had to look. It had to suffer and wrestle with suffering. That was its mission in the world. If public opinion and the medical profession and political interests would not treat addicts as people and denied them the means of finding a cure, then maybe public opinion and the medical profession and political interests might be changed by the few—pathetically few—who cared enough and believed enough and worked enough as well.

The first fruits of this care and belief and work were seen by the staff of Metropolitan Hospital when they looked out of their windows on a cold, dismal Sunday morning in March, 1959, and were surprised to see two hundred people marching back and forth in the rain. Their banners read 'East Harlem Protestant Parish,' and their signs urged 'Provide facilities for addicted adults.' The marchers had ended their morning service by walking in double file down Second Avenue to parade for an hour in silent prayer before the hospital best placed to help the addicts whom they knew. The rain poured down relentlessly, and many of the marchers were soaked and shivering by the time the benediction was asked outside the hospital gate.

For eight months before the march the Parish had tried to get a meeting on drug addiction with the Mayor; but letters, telephone calls, and telegrams went unanswered, while addicted men and women sought help the Parish could not give. A few days after the march the Mayor's assistants wrote to the Parish, but no action was taken or promised.

Six weeks went by before officials at City Hall were told that a big procession had come from a march round the Department of Hospitals and was now parading silently outside their building, too. Those six weeks had been packed with activity: the support of forty major city churches had been gained; letters to Senators and the Governor had been written by the Parish and by hundreds of its lay members; a letter requesting a meeting with the Mayor had been drafted by the Parish and sent to City Hall over the signatures of top national leaders in labour, politics, religion, and medicine; and now after a service of praise in a neighbouring church, members of the Parish, with their church and secular supporters, were marching in order 'to dramatise the need for hospital facilities for addicted adults in the city'. As reporters made their notes and television cameras whirred, a former addict, with an armful of white carnations, walked down the line, fixing them in the buttonholes of fifteen others who had once been addicts too. Like the rest of the marchers, their spirits were high because they had heard on the previous day that the Mayor would now meet with their committee.

It was a strange sight as the Mayor of New York City sat in his office, listening intently to a Harlem addict's experience. Flanked by advisers, he heard a first-hand description of the agony endured by one who had tried gallantly to overcome addiction without any medical aid. The other members of the Parish-sponsored committee testified before the Mayor and gave him concrete, clear-cut proposals. Perhaps he wondered why his staff had virtually ignored this social scourge. Or perhaps he recalled a recent letter from the Parish: 'We

have visited many state and city officials. Everywhere we have
met with courtesy. Nowhere have we met anyone with a plan.
So, in keeping with the ancient rôle of the church in ministering to those whom society neglects, we, as spokesmen for
addicted men and women, make these recommendations. . . .'
And as the Mayor turned again and again to the City
Administrator for confirmation of all the technical points
which were made, he saw that the plan before him was not
just humane but workable.

Within weeks the Mayor had agreed to act. And by November, Manhattan State Hospital had opened a fifty-five bed
research unit, and Metropolitan Hospital had opened twenty-
five beds for addicted men.

The Narcotics Office was a centre of jubilation as Carmen
Cruzado and Red Gomez duplicated hundreds of notices:

November 16, 1959

Addicted men and women can now get treatment at
Metropolitan State Hospital. This is the direct result of
the work of the winter and spring. The Metropolitan staff
seem warm, understanding, but swamped with work.
Right now, this is what a person does who wants to be
admitted:
1. *8.30 a.m. go to the Registration window.* . . .

The Parish's jubilation was justified. Carmen was right to
head her notices: ' First Step Towards Victory!' But there
were twenty-three thousand addicts in New York. More than
five hundred addicts were seeking help from the Parish every
year. And for all these there were eighty beds. It was like
having five loaves to feed five thousand people. ' That's
exactly what it's like,' said a shy narcotics worker with a
smile. ' With eighty beds, twenty-three thousand addicts, and
a whole lot of faith—what can stop us?' And as the Governor's newly appointed Narcotics Task Force met with doctors
and other experts in the state capital, it looked at first as
though nothing could stop the faith and the works that had
caused them to meet at all. For this meeting of top city,
state, and federal officials made proposals which were virtually the same as those put forward months before by the
Parish: more research facilities, hospital beds, and a long-
term after-care programme. ' What can stop us?'

The answer to the question soon emerged. It was ' Money '.

For when the bill to authorise the necessary $300,000 was sent by a reluctant State Assembly to the Governor for signature, experienced legislators thought it likely that he would not approve. So the Parish recalled Don Benedict's maxim, ' The best oil for a religious machine is sweat,' and pastors and youth group members, Councilmen and Sunday School teachers, addicts and the friends of addicts, all harnessed their faith to a vast amount of work, writing letters urging thousands of parishioners and others to put pressure on the Governor to sign:

> East Harlem Protestant Parish
> Narcotics Committee
> 2050 Second Avenue
> April 4, 1960
>
> Friends,
> . . . Our letters have been heard by the Legislature. Now let the Governor hear from us. This is the final push. The Governor has competent men around him who know little of the narcotics problem. So write, no matter what. But, if you can, write from your own experience and give good, clear reasons why the bill is a necessity.
>
> Sincerely yours,
> Norman C. Eddy, *Director*
> Seymour Ostrow, *Attorney*
> Rita Dougan, *Christian Action Co-ordinator*

Two weeks later the bill was signed.

That $300,000 was almost as important as the conversion of Red Gomez and as the life of the community with which he worked. The Parish knew that it was no more important. It knew that research and hospital beds could free men from their addiction. But it also knew that the strength to persevere could only be found—and then by no means always—in the life of a community, ' a community of acceptance '.

And it was certain that this kind of community was much more expensive than the most ambitious medical programme. For research and beds cost only money. But community cost lives. It cost the lives of pastors like Norm Eddy, who had grown to look much older than his years ; it cost the lives of laymen like Pee-Wee, whose face at twenty-three was shadowed with lines of care; it cost almost everything for those who followed Christ in ' laying down their lives for their friends '.

But the result was that some of those friends also followed Christ. Side by side with their partners in the Parish, they suffered and were crucified by the addiction which society thrust upon them; and with those who stayed beside them in their pain, they followed Christ beyond that crucifixion to what can only be called ' a resurrection '. And in that resurrection, as Norm Eddy testified before the President's Committee on Narcotics, ' they have found that the power of God has given them a new and healthy life.'

But then there are other friends also. And these, in a tragic sense, have followed Christ as well. Like him, they have suffered and been crucified; they have, as it were, descended into hell. But although their companions in the Parish share their torment, here their ' following ' has ceased. For they have remained in hell. They have not risen again. At least not yet.

23. RESURRECTION

'Looking at the Parish as a whole, what are the tangible results of all your work?' This is the invariable question which every visitor asks. Are there any real signs in the broad life of the Parish that the way of participation has led beyond the Cross to a clear-cut resurrection?

The signs are many. But we shall look at only one: and here we strike bedrock. For we may see this ultimate sign of resurrection as clearly as the first disciples saw the risen Christ.

The sign is the presence of a live organic Body: a visible body of Christians who have risen, as it were, from their East Harlem grave. It is the sign of a strong company of men and women who no longer depend mainly on their ministers, but on God, on one another, on themselves. It is the sign of a community which is giving men a vision, so that now the world is knocking on the church's door, demanding that it share its life and work.

Up four flights of stairs and along a narrow corridor to apartment 4D we find proof of a responsible, mature, adult church. Here we see that while the staff have not yet achieved their aim of 'working ourselves out of a job', nevertheless their leadership is now enriched and reinforced by experienced, imaginative lay men and women.

It is eight o'clock on Wednesday evening, and the Bible study group is about to start. Sixteen people are laughing and talking in the housing project apartment; they are an inter-racial group, and their ages range from the twenty-year-old lorry driver to the eighty-year-old lady who sits, straight-backed, with her magnifying glass poised over her Bible. This is one of twelve groups which are meeting in different Parish apartments; there are usually about ten in each group, and often non-members come. This time there are four people present who have no church connection; they have been invited by their Parish neighbours. 'C'mon there!' calls a middle-aged man to the apartment's tenant who is washing

her hair at the sink: 'We're ready to go!' Soon, amid
general applause, the chuckling woman takes her place in the
circle with one of her six children on her lap. Then the
talking subsides and everyone looks to the leader.

Joe Thomas is a church Councilman who a few weeks
before had persuaded the Parish to hold a political meeting
at which two City Assemblyman candidates spoke to a big
audience in 106th Street church. His interest in politics has its
roots in such study groups as this. 'Let us pray,' says Joe. . . .
And after his prayer they read Luke's tenth chapter aloud;
and then they re-read the last few verses—about Martha, busy
making a meal for Jesus, while Mary, her sister, sits listening
intently at his feet. Half a dozen questions on the background
to the story are put to the pastor who sits on a cushion on the
floor. Then silence . . . A man whose work gets him up each
day at four o'clock begins to nod in his chair, until Joe
Thomas sums up the essence of the story with, 'Wasn't it
like this? Martha, she was glad to see the Lord. She was
happy to see the Lord. But she got so busy in the kitchen with
all them pots and pans, she didn't take time to sit down with
him, and entertain him. I can understand that. But then she
didn't take time neither to be entertained *by* him. That was
the trouble, I guess. What d'you think?'

'I just don't know what was troubling Martha, poor girl,'
says a young mother. 'What does the lectionary say?' She
looks through the Parish Bible study notes, and waves of
laughter greet her exclamation. 'My! It's clearer here than
in the Bible!' She reads the notes aloud: 'Service by itself
becomes hollow if we don't take time to come close to Jesus
in prayer.' 'That's right,' she thinks aloud. 'I guess we're in
the kitchen, like Martha; and we must take time to be with
the Lord. . . .'

'Maybe so,' says the apartment's tenant with a frown, 'but
what d'you do when you got five or six kids all wanting
something at the same time? How 'bout that? What d'you
do?'

'Well I get *mad*!' says one mother, 'and sometimes I
hammer 'em hard!'

'That's how it is,' nods a bright-eyed Negro woman.
'When kids are like that, well, sometimes I feel like screamin'
blue murder! But I guess '—she shakes her head thoughtfully—'I guess I should just go into a room, and shut the

door, and be quiet for a while, and maybe pray: like " Lord
I just don't know what to do. What'll I do, Lord? You tell
me." Then I reckon the Lord helps us. In just a minute.
Then we can come back to the kids and tell them what to do.
And, you know, they know you're different somehow. . . .'

A murmur of agreement comes from most of the group, as
though they know that this is true from their experience.

For nearly an hour the discussion centres around the
figure of Martha; and it is a striking fact that the group's
discoveries are very like those made a few days earlier in the
staff's study of the same passage when advantage was taken
of a knowledge of the Greek text and of the views of the early
Fathers, of Martin Luther, and of modern scholars: and this
fact does not minimise the value of the staff's hard work, for it
is just such work which has equipped the laity with their present grasp of the Gospel and their mature Christian judgment.

Suddenly one of the men interrupts the pastor's remarks
about Martha. ' All right, all right! Maybe Martha *was* distracted by her work. But Mary was distracted too! She was
so distracted by the Lord being there, she couldn't think of
anything else.'

There is a growl from an armchair in a corner of the room.
' She was a hypocrite!' a deep bass voice declares. This is the
first time that one of the four newcomers has spoken. He
rubs his chin with the back of a hairy hand. ' I reckon Mary
was kinda hypocrite just sitting there. Like some folks who's
always going to church. There's plenty hypocrites in the
church. . . .' Another newcomer looks round uneasily, perhaps expecting protests from the group. Instead, murmurs
of assent greet the non-churchgoer. Looking faintly surprised,
he goes on: ' I think you don't need to go to church to be
close to God. . . .' And he looks round. Again, church members' heads nod slowly in agreement. There is a pause. . . .
' And yet, y'know . . . It's been a long time since I was in a
gathering like this. Somehow I stayed away from this kind of
gathering. Don't know why . . . But . . .' He hesitates. . . .
' You remember what Jesus said about " When two or three is
gathered together, there am I "? Well, right now there's a
strong feeling like God is with us. . . . I feel God is with us.
I reckon that way you get strength in a gathering.'

It is nearly eleven now, and the session is reaching its climax. Joe Thomas reads the story from the Bible once again. Then, after a pause, he says, 'Let's pray.' Everyone bows in a circle of silence which for several thoughtful moments is unbroken. Then comes the most moving part of the evening as now one and now another offers prayer. There is no sense of strain. There is a great sense of reality. Perhaps one ought to say there is a sense of God. And that sense of God is deepened when, quietly and sincerely, the final prayer is sung:

> Breathe on me, Breath of God,
> Fill me with life anew,
> That I may love what thou dost love,
> And do what thou wouldst do.

And as the verse is repeated still more softly, the newcomer's deep bass voice joins in:

> That I may love what thou dost love,
> And do what thou wouldst do.

Such groups are visible signs of 'resurrection'. Scattered throughout the Parish in new housing projects and crumbling tenements, they bring new life and vision to church members and their friends.

At first, most lay members were not enthusiastic at the idea of having Bible study groups; but when the staff persisted, some of them reluctantly agreed to start. They began by telling Letty Russell (one of two ordained women on the staff) that 'Paul said that women shouldn't be preachers!' But after one session on Paul's first letter to the church at Corinth, with its straight talk on Christian disobedience, they were astonished to discover that 'This guy Paul's got our number!' Soon they were discussing their deepest moral failures and their most secret hopes; they were exposing themselves to the Scriptures and to one another as they had not done before; and the result was an influx of strong new life into the church. It was a resurrection life which was clearly given not only by the Gospels and not only by the study groups but by the God who came to men through both.

With this discovery many have turned eagerly to the daily Bible readings and the notes which the Parish prepares: some read them on the subway, some read them in the kitchen,

some read them with their families each day. These readings
are the basis both for study groups and for Sunday sermons;
so when people come to the Wednesday groups, they already
have questions in their minds, or they have answers to the
questions of their friends. And when next Sunday they listen
to the preacher—who knows the main concerns which have
emerged in all the groups—their response has its roots in
serious reflection on the sermon's principal theme.

The effect of this multiple exposure to the Gospel has been
profound. It has brought the Parish as a whole much nearer
God. It has deepened the desire of 'ordinary' members to
make the Gospel live. It is giving them strength and wisdom
and direction, as is proved beyond doubt in action.

Sometimes that action is quite undramatic; like the work
with Parish school children. But it is hard work: hard in a
way that demands a lot of time and thought and a good deal
of responsibility. Yet this is one way that gives signs of
'resurrection'.

One pastor's wife has developed strong relations between
the children's homes and their schools by serving on the local
five-member School Board; another gives a course for older
school girls in her home where they face their fears and
superstitions in matters of sex and marriage, and see something of the possibilities of happiness in married life; a third
leads a parents' group which seeks a better understanding of
their children's needs and of how to cope with common
family crises.

Such work is integrated with that of the Parish laity who,
for example, provide most of the leaders (including all three
presidents) of the local Parent-Teacher Associations. Equally
important for most of the children whose hopes are blocked
by wretched schooling is the children's library and the
remedial reading clinic which the Parish has developed; these
strike at the roots of future frustrations and crime and unemployment in the life of the average local child who is two to
six grades behind children in less crowded schools. Over the
years such work as this has inspired a new attitude to life in
scores of boys and girls, some of whom have won their way
to college through the Parish College Programme, and are

now engaged in social work, in counselling delinquent boys, while one, a young Negro with a brilliant academic record, has recently been ordained. In terms of persevering effort and concern this broad-based educational work is as demanding as it is rewarding.

But Christian action can be more than rewarding. It can be dangerous and costly. It can be far more costly for the laity than for the staff: that is why it calls for lay men and women with strong God-centred lives. For, as one church member writes, ' Life isn't easy, even in the church. Jesus had faith, but he died on the Cross. And being in the church does not mean doing what you want. It means following Christ by helping God do what *he* wants.' And because this deeply Christian attitude is shared by many with an equally adult faith, the Parish as a whole is willing to take costly action: for it has found that tackling the greatest dangers often brings the richest rewards—the graver the chance of crucifixion, the higher the hope of resurrection.

For example, the reporting of police brutality is, in the minds of most parishioners, like jumping into a busy concrete mixer. They have seen innocent men shot dead by patrolmen ; they themselves may have been put through agonies in a local police station ; but they are afraid to report what has occurred because of the likelihood of ruthless reprisals. Even when thirty young boys were beaten and tortured in order to get a confession to a murder, it seemed unlikely that any resident would have the courage to protest.

So when the Parish faced the fact that this abuse of privilege mattered intensely to God, when it compiled a detailed analysis of cases of brutality, and when it asked for volunteers to face no less a person than the Police Commissioner, many said that it would take a miracle to get any witnesses at all. They were right. But what they did not realise was that the miracle had already occurred. For when two Parish pastors, Randy Hammond and Norm Eddy, drove to the Commissioner's office, there were packed into their station wagon a total of fifteen residents who were willing, despite their fears, to testify.

Into the panelled room at Police Headquarters came Commissioner Stephen P. Kennedy, a stenographer, and five aides. They sat down at the big mahogany table, and Kennedy looked round at the varied company, and said, 'Now who's to testify?' Randy Hammond rose to his feet: 'Before we start, Mr. Commissioner, may we open the meeting with prayer?' For an instant it looked as though the police chief might be nonplussed. But only for an instant. 'Well . . . Yes, Reverend. Sure. Let's do that.' The portraits of three dozen past Commissioners looked down at the assorted heads bowed in prayer ; one wonders if they looked surprised ; more probably they wore approving expressions as Randy Hammond's prayer recalled the vocation that was theirs : ' " Except the Lord keep the city, the watchman stays awake in vain." Look on us, O Lord, each with our different ministry, but each seeking the peace of thy city. . . .' When the prayer was done, there was silence for a while as Kennedy studied the back of his hand. Then came a keen question-and-answer period, with witnesses testifying for three full hours, at the end of which concrete proposals were laid before the Commissioner, who there and then rejected some, accepted others, and restricted his comments on the need for reform at the local police station to, 'You'll be hearing from me soon.'

The telephone rang in the Hammonds' apartment three or four days later. 'That Reverend Hammond? Inspector Kahn speaking. Can you come round and meet the new Captain of the station?' The new Captain was a Baptist lay preacher. He believed that ' the Bible is a moral force more powerful to change men than a whole roomful of truncheons '.

What difference did Captain Jensen's coming make? 'Well,' said a disgusted patrolman to Randy Hammond, ' we can't swear at line-up any more.' But there were other things that patrolmen could not do. Brutality declined markedly. And while, since 1948, there had never been less than two lives lost through irresponsible police shootings each year, there has not been one such shooting since the new Captain came ; not one life has been lost.

' I am come that they might have life,' the Parish had read in its group Bible studies, ' and that they might have it more abundantly.' Christ's words had more than spiritual meaning. For this life, this ' resurrection life ', was coming in very concrete ways as the church obeyed the divine command to make the Gospel visible to men.

Not that all men were willing to have the church demonstrate its Gospel. But the more ruthless the opposition, the faster the church matured. Violence and abuse and threats of eviction all appeared to serve one purpose: the renewal of the church's life.

On a bitterly cold Sunday in January 1960, the worship in 100th Street church had reached the point at which subjects were offered for prayer. 'There's no heat at all in these five tenements,' said Pura Rodriguez, a Puerto Rican with six children and a sea-going husband. 'We must do something for the tenants and we must pray for the landlord. He's been to every apartment and he's pushed us around. He knows we have no heat because he's seen the ice on the hallway walls. And he says, " If you don't pay more rent, you'll be evicted!." The church has got to act.'

Her pastor, Wendell Elmendorf, knew what she meant by 'the church'. She did not mean 'they'; some remote authority with power. She meant 'us'; her pastor, her church friends, herself; a local community with power; power of an intangible, increasingly realistic kind. 'We'll talk more of this after the service,' said Elmendorf. 'Right now we'll do as Pura says and make our intercessions for the landlord. Let us pray. . . .'

When the service was over, ten members stayed behind and made a circle of chairs beside the Lord's table. As they bowed in prayer for their landlord and themselves, some drew their coats and scarves more tightly round them, for the storefront was rented from the same landlord and had no heating at all. For an hour they discussed the issue, and finally decided to keep on praying at home, to get legal advice, and to call a tenants' meeting for Wednesday evening.

Next day five or six church youths pushed invitations under 165 apartment doors; and two days later seventy-three tenants met in the church.

'My windows are broken and the rain and the wind and the snow blows through,' said a frail old lady who had neither the strength nor the funds to make repairs.

'My baby boy's in hospital with pneumonia,' a young lorry driver said. 'There's just no heat at all.'

'And we're on Welfare,' said a grizzled church Council-man. 'We got to heat our apartment by lighting the stove. Costs us thirty dollars instead of three dollars for cooking. Can't go on. We gotta do something or we'll freeze.'

'What about it, Mark?' asked Elmendorf, looking at the lean young man beside him. Mark Lane was a local lawyer who was giving his help free of charge: and on his advice they did three things. They prepared and signed a protest addressed to the Department of Buildings; they appointed two representatives from each of the tenements to compile a detailed report on the state of the 165 apartments; and—this was the hardest decision to take—they decided that five tenants should each serve a summons on the landlord. 'Where could we go if we was evicted?' came the urgent question from a man with five young children. The answer was hard to give. Any tenant could be turned out on a purely technical point. And it was almost impossible to find a new home: especially in the depths of winter.

So they prayed. Church members and non-church-members prayed together. And the summonses were served: the protests were posted: and the carefully compiled reports on conditions were sent off. And then they prayed again, and waited for results.

Their wait was brief. The choir was rehearsing in the church a few nights later. With their backs to the rough-hewn cross on the wall, they faced down the aisle towards the street door as they sang:

> He is King of kings.
> He is Lord of lords.
> Jesus Christ, the first and . . .

The younger members of the choir stopped singing as the door banged open and a stranger, with a severe manner, gazed at them intently before advancing on Elmendorf. He handed him an envelope: 'Eviction notice, Reverend. You got to be out in thirty days.'

At just about that moment, three floors above their heads, a gun was being levelled at a middle-aged woman—a Mrs. Day —who stood petrified at her door.

'*Take* it!' urged the landlord, thrusting the eviction notice at her. 'You can't refuse. And if you do, this gun's going off.'

She took it. And then she collapsed.

As soon as the man was gone, her terrified daughter ran up the stairs to beat on a door which bore the Parish label—a handclasp on the background of a cross and the words, 'Welcome in the name of Christ.' Pura Rodriguez opened the door to the child and then hurried down the stairs to help her neighbour. In the next few days they became such firm friends that Pura gave her the courage to protect her family by serving a summons on the landlord for assault. Together they discussed the issue; together they prayed about it; together they went to every hearing in the court. 'In the early days,' says Elmendorf, 'I would have gone with her. But now we've reached a level of church maturity at which it is obvious that Pura has a pastoral ministry, too.' It was the ministry of lay men and women like Pura that was carrying the Gospel out of the church, and inspiring others with the Biblical vision of a people who 'let the oppressed go free': a vision which took them—reluctantly but inevitably—out into the once frightening world, with its city courts and its seemingly all-powerful Rent Administration.

'What are the complaints?' asked the Deputy Rent Administrator, looking up from his desk at Elmendorf, who sat beside the landlord. The pastor looked inquiringly round the thirteen tenants who were packed into the office, and restrained a smile as two mothers tried to stifle the cries of the babies they had had to bring. Despite the presence of the landlord and the real risk of violence and eviction that their evidence involved, the tenants poured out a stream of complaints: about ice-cold apartments, garbage, rats, fouled corridors, and the stench from useless toilets . . . 'That's enough!' cried the Deputy, with a frown of disgust. 'I don't want all the gruesome details.' But he was not to be spared; for a woman was groping gingerly in her bag as she announced deliberately,

'Only this morning I caught a rat in the toilet. Just a minute. I got it right here for you to see. Here it . . .'

The Deputy leaped to his feet, wide-eyed, with an anxious arm outraised: 'Put it back! That's just what I don't want you to do. Put it back, I tell you.'

Looking vaguely hurt, the woman replaced the struggling rat in the bag, and the excited cries of the children died away.

' Now,' the Deputy went on, casting an uneasy eye at the mother who was feeding her child from a jar on the edge of his desk, ' What has the landlord to say?'

' I have done everything I could do,' came the answer, and the landlord launched into a catalogue of questionable claims about his care of the property and about his tenants' faults. To his surprise, he was answered by a storm of contradictions from those who were learning to defend their basic rights. And as babies howled and the landlord shouted, the Deputy tried in vain to quell the mounting storm of protest which was rising to a crescendo when the mother by the desk flung out her arm in passionate dissent and accidentally dashed her soupy cereal over the administrator's desk.

When thirteen apologetic pairs of hands had finished wiping baby food off Rent Department forms, the Deputy returned from his refuge by the wall to declare:

" If we find that what the tenants say is true, the landlord must make improvements right away. If he does not, we'll have the rents reduced.'

Heartened by the courage they had found to face authority, the tenants returned to their ice-cold homes and waited for results.

There were none. The landlord took no action. Nor did he act when the Magistrates' Court heard the evidence of thirty-four resolute tenants and found him guilty on eight counts. So there was just one thing left to do. They had tried persuasion. They had tried negotiation. Reluctantly, they had tried the law. All that was left was direct action. That action was planned after Sunday worship on March 13th 1960.

Three days later, the manager of a luxurious Greenwich Village apartment building was dismayed to hear the tramp of feet and the singing of hymns as an East Harlem picket line marched back and forth outside. Their placards read, ' Mr. Robinson—Heat & Hot Water, Please '; ' Fix Our Windows '; ' It's Mighty Cold Inside '. In the icy March wind, the twenty-one tenants and two ministers marched in orderly procession for ninety minutes. ' Sure I'm cold,' one of them answered a passer-by with a laugh. ' Feels just like my apartment!' One immaculate resident stood on the brick-and-glass doorstep, asking in amazement, 'You mean that kind of landlord lives in *our* building?' And a dignified woman remarked to Pura Rodriguez, 'I hope it shames him into doing something about those awful buildings.'

It did. Or, rather, what did it was the combination of the picketing, the court appearances, the mounting number of summonses, and above all, the fact that the landlord was confronted with a community of Christians whose prayerfulness and faith were matched by their humour and grit.

Soon the garbage was being collected, the doors and windows were repaired, and a $26,000 oil burner was giving automatic heat to all five tenements.

Yet results went deeper than that. The tenants had become a community. They belonged to one another as never before. Moreover, the Gospel had come alive for a number of non-church tenants: they joined the Bible study groups, and some began the ten-week class for full church membership.

But it has worked both ways. There were some tenants belonging to the Parish who had gained a greater vision of the need to work the faith into the fabric of everyday life. Their enthusiasm for the Bible study groups remained as keen as ever ; but now they were also eager to fight for better, cleaner local politics, and so oppose injustice on a material as well as on a spiritual level—or, as they said, ' on a Christian level '.

Their decision to work on political problems was made right at the start of the 1960 election campaign ; and in some uncertainty they looked to their pastors for a lead.

They looked in vain.

Six years before it had been the Group which had led the all but successful bid to defeat the district's Congressman. But now there were others who could lead. The staff's main job was the strengthening of the church, ' the training of Christ's people for *their* work of ministry' in worship, evangelism, politics. So when the Group was urged to supervise a Parish political programme, the majority refused point-blank.

To some this seemed like madness. For the first time in years there was a chance that Negroes and Puerto Ricans, as well as Italians, might gain real representation at state level, for Mark Lane, the lawyer who had worked for the tenants on 100th Street, was opposing the local Italian-dominated Demo-

cratic machine. During seven years' practice in East Harlem,
Lane had championed the cause of many who could not defend themselves, and now he was State Assemblyman candidate for the Reform Democrats who were out to break the
regular Democratic party's monopoly of power in New York.
Apart from Lane's proven integrity, it was clear that he shared
the aims of the Parish in such matters as housing, education,
narcotics ; and unlike the regular Democratic Club, the political club which he hoped to form would be open—in fact as
well as in theory—to anyone of any racial group. 'Will we
let this chance slip by?' demanded one of the staff. 'We will
have an active club that shares our goals and a strong laity to
join us in the fight. Why don't we give a lead?' The answer
was clear : 'The laity is certainly strong. They will grow
stronger if they take the lead themselves.'

So lay members could not settle down behind a Parish-
sponsored programme. They were faced with a choice. They
could give Lane's club merely nominal support. Or they
could give it active leadership. Within weeks the choice was
made.

They attended a weekly 'programme of political education' which was led by Norm Eddy and held in his home.
This was not a form of indoctrination in which the laity were
told what they ought to do : it was a way of offering them a
detached view of the political scene, and of providing a basis
for discussions which would help *them* decide what they ought
to do. In the Eddys' apartment they met local political
leaders and compared their aims and especially their achievements. Far into the night they drank black coffee and explored the complex issues. They talked politics, prayed politics, learned about the ugly side of city politics, and determined to act on the conclusions of their Bible study theme :
'Unto us a Child is born, unto us a Son is given, and the
government shall be upon his shoulder. . . .'

Soon, twenty-five lay men and women were helping Lane
start a Reform Democrat club, and before long some eighty
of their non-church friends had been roused from political
apathy to work for the club as well. Two months before the
June primary elections, Parish members had been elected to
most of the club's positions of leadership : several were on the
Executive Committee, one was Committee Treasurer, and the

volatile Carlos Rios—104th Street's Puerto Rican lay pastor—had been elected permanent Chairman.

Four weeks before the primaries all the spare time that these lay people had was being spent campaigning for Lane's Assembly nomination and for Carlos's election as Democratic State Committeeman. Joined now by some of the ministers, they mingled with the crowds around the loudspeaker truck and elaborated Lane's straight talk and Carlos's flood of Spanish. They led a vigorous registration drive, and made such an impact with their obvious sincerity that they gained four thousand new voters, many of whom were Puerto Ricans whose fear of the literacy test had held them back from registering for over thirty years. And when the primaries actually came, they hounded those four thousand from their homes, scoured the streets for additional voters, and one of them who chose to stand near the voting centre fixed all those who passed with a steely eye, and repeated over and over again, 'Hey! Vote for Carlos! Hear?'

Carlos won. And in the November election, despite intense opposition from Republicans and regular Democrats, Mark Lane also won. He had a majority of 3,400; and that margin of victory was given by an overwhelming vote in the Parish area.

It was certainly a triumph for Lane, for Carlos, and for the Parish members and the friends they had inspired. The exclusive, entrenched Democratic machine had been defeated by an insurgent candidate; one of New York's strongest political bosses had been beaten by a Puerto Rican; and at last the urgent problems of all East Harlem's social groups—segregation, addiction, exploitation—would be voiced where political decisions were actually made.

No wonder all this grips the imagination of many non-church-members. When 'ordinary' men and women not only storm the gates of heaven, as the Parish does in its worship and its weekly Bible groups, but when they gain so much from that assault that they storm the gates of the world as well and win campaigns for better schools, police, housing, representation, then they have become what we have called the bedrock sign of resurrection, a flesh-and-blood expression of God's love for the whole of life. And it is not surprising that the world is turning to them as to a light in the dark.

It would be absurd to claim that after only fifteen years East Harlem as a whole is turning to the church. Far from it. Of the one hundred and ten passers-by who recently were asked their views of the Parish just over half did not even know what the Parish was. They had other things to occupy their minds. Rats still ran riot in their crumbling tenements, and children still went hungry and had insufficient clothes. New housing projects might be rising everywhere, but addicts still died on rooftops from an overdose of drugs, and the danger from armed thieves still made elderly tenants say, 'I tell you, I'm afraid just all the time.' Perhaps those who were questioned were preoccupied with deeper tensions: the estrangement of children from parents, the hatred of race for race, the bitter resentment against a society which still seems to stand, like a merciless foe, waiting for another chance to strike. At all events it is a fact that great numbers in the district which is served by the Parish do not even begin to see in the church the answer to the frustrations which still corrode their lives.

And yet it is also true that, in one way or another, hosts of men and women *are* turning to the church. There are many who speak of the four congregations or the farm or the narcotics centre as men might speak of an oasis in a desert. And some of them are turning to this 'oasis' because they want to share in a life and a vision which extends far beyond the church's membership, not just to the Parishes whose growth has been inspired in Cleveland and Chicago, in Scotland, England, and India, but, far more significant for local men and women, to the farthest corners of the strange world of East Harlem where life has begun to make sense for outcast, broken men as well as for strong, aggressive groups. It is the biggest crisis in the life of one such lawless group that typifies, in miniature, that world's response to the preaching and living of a Gospel that accepts men just as they are and makes their hearts and homes and neighbourhoods as whole as they themselves allow.

The Enchanters reluctantly admired the Parish, though no one would have guessed it. They were one of the most feared gangs in New York City, and their empire spread through lower Manhattan, the Bronx, and Brooklyn, and over the river to New Jersey. They were strongest of all in East Harlem, and they symbolised East Harlem's plight. Their members were frustrated by the colour of their skin and their lack of education and work ; they believed that the battle with society was futile, that they were bound to lose ; and so they tried to escape life's emptiness in the harsh world of the gang. They broke into local stores, they took wild joyrides in stolen cars, they engaged other gangs in battles which cleared the streets as if by magic while a hundred young men fought with switchblades and pistols and zip-guns and clubs and knives.

Their local meeting place was a candy store run by *La Vieja*—the Old Lady. There, on 100th Street, the leaders smoked endless cigarettes, listened to the jukebox, and planned the next attack on the Dragons or the Latin Gents. Sometimes they talked with *La Vieja's* godson, the likeable thirty-year-old Ramon Diaz who belonged to the Parish church across the street.

For over ten years some of the Enchanters had watched that church develop. They had seen it get involved in what for them was real life—the hard world of racketeers and addicts and police. They had seen its striking triumphs ; they had seen its dismal failures ; and failure meant as much to them as any triumph did, for both proved the fact that the church not only worked but, above all, that it *cared*. It cared enough to keep on standing by the ' hopeless ' addict. It cared enough to keep on helping hundreds who never joined its ranks. It cared enough to visit a jailed Enchanter and to write him month after month, year after year, so that instead of falling apart, as do most men in for ' twenty years or life ', he learned a trade, discovered the Gospel, and became himself a man who cared.

From behind stacked cigarette cartons in the store window they had watched local people like themselves slowly change, so that now they saw the church's caring expressed not just by its college-bred immigrants but by those who had grown up in East Harlem, by those who had once been frustrated and afraid, by those who were now a strong, live community which seemed to know what life was for.

'Say, Ramon,' Boppo's voice was strained, and Ramon Diaz looked up inquiringly from the back of the store where he was opening a crate. Boppo Cruz, in grey leather jacket and jeans, was standing with six other Enchanters, all of whom looked strangely grave. 'Say, Ramon. There's something we gotta say.' Ramon put his hammer down, picked his way between cartons and crates, and then looked with interest at the burly leader of the gang.

'You come to take me away?' he asked with a smile. The Enchanters remained serious.

'Ramon,' said Boppo. 'It's this way. . . .' He ran a black hand through his crinkly hair. 'We kinda need some help. You see . . . We wanna go social.'

There was a heavy pause while Ramon frowned unbelievingly, and then slowly tipped his cap on to the back of his head.

'*Social?*' he asked. 'Did you say "*social*"?' Perhaps he was remembering the time when these Enchanters fired volley after volley at the Dragons from a hallway down the street; or perhaps he was recalling the day when two of the gang were shot and two more stabbed outside his own church door.

'That's it,' said Boppo, and all the others nodded: 'Social.'

Ramon's broad smile came back; but he was unconvinced. He knew the district and the gang too well.

'Go 'way,' he said good-humouredly, turning to get back to his work. 'You guys don't mean it.'

But Boppo and his men were adamant. They made Ramon sit down while they told him that the gang wanted to give up stealing and street fights and narcotics; and they wanted the Parish to help them go straight.

Ramon put them off. He had a great love for people, and a deep, clear trust in God, but this was enough to try the strongest faith. He knew that scores of hardened criminals had found help from the church. He knew that each week more than twelve new addicts were helped to some extent by the church. But that the leaders of the legendary Enchanters

should now stand, as it were, knocking on the church's door
. . . this just could not happen.

Yet finally, when the gang had persisted for a week, Ramon summoned up the faith to say, 'Well, I'll go see Norm.' Norm Eddy was as doubtful as Ramon. And 100th Street Church Council was more doubtful still. Nor was this surprising ; for however much the church believed that it should accept all who came to its door, must there not be a limit in the case of a gang whose history was deeply stained with crime and violence and blood?

But when the vote was taken, the church doors were not shut ; and a few evenings later thirty-two Enchanters were packed into the small church hall and were working out with Ramon Diaz the basis for a strong, non-warring gang.

Within weeks they had a code as demanding as that of a fighting gang ; they had given up their famous name and were calling themselves the Conservatives ; and they had taken the crucial step of giving up all their guns. Now they had no arsenal. They were powerless to fight. They had taken a momentous step of faith.

And at once there came a challenge from the Dragons. The battle was to be the next night. This was the time of real decision. Some of them had sold their guns ; some had thrown them into the river ; some had buried them, just in case. All that day, and the following morning and afternoon, Ramon Diaz talked with the members of the gang individually and in tense groups at the back of *La Vieja's* store. Most, including Boppo their leader, stood by their decision. But a few went down to the basement where the guns had been buried, and when the Dragons reached the corner of 100th Street, they were met by a hail of bullets which whined down among them from a housing project roof. All but one of the attackers were arrested within minutes, for the police had been notified ; two of those in the rooftop ambush were sentenced to five years in jail, and the rest were left wondering if there were any real alternative to war.

'It's not easy,' said Norm Eddy, looking round the congregation which included twelve Conservatives. 'When a gang comes into the neighbourhood with their pieces, you want to fight back, and yet something tells you it's wrong. But you're afraid of being called a punk. It needs courage to go beyond that. It needs a special kind of courage—the courage to stand up for God. And if you do that, maybe people will call you a punk for six months, but then finally they'll turn to you and look up to you. But it will be hard.'

It was certainly hard. Some church members insisted that the gang had betrayed their trust; they wondered if they should in fact be barred from the church hall. But after a few days' uncertainty the gang had become more determined than before. They urged Ramon Diaz to help them with their plans, they persisted relentlessly in seeking Eddy's aid, and they stopped other members of the Parish on the street and earnestly argued their case. The world was no longer 'knocking on the church's door'. Now it was hammering hard.

And it prevailed. With the help of Ramon and Norm Eddy (who held informal meetings several times a week), they worked hard to get a place of their own where they could make the incredibly complex transition from a fighting gang to a strong, creative club. They spent months earning money to rent their own clubroom, and what they raised was matched by friends of the Parish who wanted to give their help; until one autumn day, on upper First Avenue, passers-by stopped to stare at the result.

Outside a storefront between The Veteran Bar and a plumbing store, each of the thirty members was taking turns to climb a rickety ladder, dip his hand in a tin of silver paint, and then press his palm on the store's big black signboard. Soon the whole length of the board was covered with shining silver prints, symbols of a radically new way of life, a way that could end finger-printing for good. Boppo Cruz stood back to survey the result, unconsciously stroking the knife scar by his eye; then he led the other members into the clubroom, and the door swung to behind them.

For some, that storefront base became the source of a full and rounded life, with its self-imposed discipline, its rugged recreation programme, its community service, and its opportunities for education and for finding jobs through Ramon Diaz who now worked full time for the club.

For a few, this rounded life meant more than jobs, recreation, and service: it meant the Christian community: it meant God. Once a week, six or seven of them got together with a layman, and for two or three hours they studied the Bible and argued and listened and prayed. And slowly, as Ramon Diaz says, 'some found a new loyalty—Jesus Christ and his church.'

These few had discovered the secret of the church's life which they had once seen only from the window of a store. It gave them the courage which Norm Eddy had described, the courage to live so differently that people would mock at them, but 'finally they'll turn to you and look up to you.'

They did. Recruits came forward, asking to join the club. Among them were members of other fighting gangs, including the war lords of the Dragons and the Latin Gents. And by the summer of 1961 the Conservatives could rightly claim that 'we have reached our goal, and the horror of gang war has been eliminated among ourselves, and it has dropped off throughout the neighbourhood and beyond the borders of East Harlem. . . .'

'The church is all right for old women and kids. It's not for me,' Boppo had said years ago. It seems this is no longer so. The church is for him. And he knows it.

He knows it because, almost against its will, the church had exposed itself to all that the gang might have done to its buildings, its fabric, its good name, its members. He knows it because this exposure, this involvement in the world, this 'being buried like a grain of wheat', has borne real fruit by leading him, and many hundreds like him, to a strong, creative life. Incarnation, as his pastor puts it, has led beyond the cross to resurrection. God's guarantee is being honoured.

And Boppo believes that one day it will be honoured even in the lives of such deeply disillusioned men as Julio, his ex-Enchanter friend.

Before sunset every evening Julio climbs to a grimy tenement roof. 'He used to let me go with him,' says Boppo, ' but that was before the gun fight with the Dragons.' After that fight Julio dodged the police and reburied his gun ; but he did not rejoin the Conservatives. Neither did he join another arm of the Enchanters. He joined nothing. He walked alone. Life

was so futile and the world's claws so sharp that the only
answer he could see was to build a wall around himself—to
belong to nothing, to be loyal to nothing, to give himself to
nothing. Except for just one thing. . . .

When he comes out on the rooftop, he pauses and looks
around to be quite sure he is alone. Then he hears a welcome
sound, and his face is eager as he walks towards the pigeon
house, and stands for a while just looking at the birds.

At this moment the roof is his domain. He is alone above
the din and squalor of the street: alone beside the pigeon
house which he built from salvaged wood. It belongs to him.
He made it.

And the birds . . . They flutter their wings and jockey for
position as he comes near their home. He looks at them
keenly to be sure they are all right; perhaps they are 'just
birds', but they are his, really *his*. He loosens the catch on
the little door, slips his hand inside, and soon he holds a grey-
white pigeon to his cheek, stroking it and murmuring softly,
as a mother might croon to her child.

The sun is low in the sky as he straightens up and holds the
bird before him in one careful hand. Gently, he swings it
forward through an arc, and then his fingers part, and it
spreads its wings and soars up high, looking almost white in
the last bright rays of the sun.

He stands there, silent, gazing . . . his arm still raised
towards the sky as if reaching up to grasp God's Spirit as it
comes down upon him like a dove. He is grave, indescribably
so ; as grave as the young pastor who back in 1948 turned
away from the first storefront church to the street, and said of
the wilderness that he had come to serve, 'This is my home.
This is where I belong.' Maybe one day Julio will turn
instead from the street to the church, and will say of this
community which has also learned to serve, 'This is *my*
home. This is where *I* belong.'

The chances seem very much against it. But then it does
not all depend on chance.

LETTERS AND PAPERS FROM PRISON
DIETRICH BONHOEFFER

These documents, smuggled out of prison under the noses of the Gestapo, have a clear and shining unity.

LET MY PEOPLE GO
ALBERT LUTHULI

The autobiography of the great South African leader—awarded the Nobel Peace Prize in 1961.

LE MILIEU DIVIN
PIERRE TEILHARD DE CHARDIN

The author of *The Phenomenon of Man* discusses man also in his relation to God. A biographical essay is included.

GOD'S FROZEN PEOPLE
MARK GIBBS AND T. RALPH MORTON

'A most important and stimulating book . . . clear and revolutionary thinking about the role of the laity.'

Archdeacon of London

MERE CHRISTIANITY
C. S. LEWIS

'He has a quite unique power for making theology an attractive, exciting and fascinating quest.' *Times Literary Supplement*

THE PSALMS: *A New Translation*

'A very impressive rendering. I am filled with admiration for the translators' achievements and have nothing but praise for it.' *Professor H. H. Rowley*

PHOENIX AT COVENTRY
SIR BASIL SPENCE

'A rare attempt to see how the architect's mind works in solving complicated problems of construction, economics and theology.' ILLUSTRATED, *Times Literary Supplement*

ALSO AVAILABLE
IN THE FONTANA RELIGIOUS SERIES

GOD, SEX AND WAR
Introduced by DONALD MacKINNON

'A magnificently honest and wise attempt to face certain of the great problems of our time.' *William Barclay*

NAUGHT FOR YOUR COMFORT
TREVOR HUDDLESTON

'A noble book, a superb book, to be read by anyone who cares about race or human relations.' *The Guardian*

THE TRUE AND LIVING GOD
TREVOR HUDDLESTON

'. . . a prophetic testimony to a living God . . . by one of the great figures of our age.' *Church Times*

THE MAN NEXT TO ME
ANTHONY BARKER

'An altogether exceptional exposition of modern missionary endeavour.' *Trevor Huddleston*

FAITH, FACT AND FANTASY
Introduced by C. F. D. MOULE

Four Cambridge lectures on the interrelation of science, psychiatry and religion today.

A MAN CALLED PETER
CATHERINE MARSHALL

The famous biography of Peter Marshall—one of the best loved ministers of our time.

'Will do good to everyone who reads it.' *Hugh Redwood*

MR. JONES, MEET THE MASTER
PETER MARSHALL

The sermons and prayers of the man who became Chaplain to the United States Senate. Over 350,000 copies sold.